The Myth of Consumerism

Conrad Lodziak

Pluto Press

LONDON • STERLING, VIRGINIA

First published 2002 by Pluto Press
345 Archway Road, London N6 5AA
and 22883 Quicksilver Drive,
Sterling, VA 20166–2012, USA

www.plutobooks.com

British Library Cataloguing in Publication Data
A catalogue record for this book is available from the British Library

Library of Congress Cataloging in Publication Data
Lodziak, Conrad.
    The myth of consumerism / Conrad Lodziak.
        p. cm.
    Includes bibliographical references and index.
    ISBN 0–7453–1761–8 (hardback) — ISBN 0–7453–1760–X (paperback)
    1. Consumption (Economics)—Social aspects. 2. Consumer behavior. 3.
Consumers—Psychology. 4. Materialism. I. Title.
    HB801 .L62 2002
    306.3—dc21
                                                    2001006379

ISBN 0 7453 1761 8 hardback
ISBN 0 7453 1760 X paperback

11   10   09   08   07   06   05   04   03   02
10   9   8   7   6   5   4   3   2   1

Designed and produced for Pluto Press by
Chase Publishing Services, Fortescue, Sidmouth EX10 9QG
Typeset from disk by Stanford DTP Services, Towcester
Printed in the European Union by TJ International, Padstow, England

Contents

Acknowledgements

Thanks are due to Finn Bowring, Steve Brown, Dave Burton, Kev Clifton, Lee Cummings, Adrian Elliott, John Fryer, Françoise Gollain, Ian Goodley, Steve Harper, Josephine Logan, Shaun McMann, Gabe Mythen, Ian Orton, Gary Robinson and Nick Scuffins. Special thanks are due to André Gorz, who has been inspirational for so long, and to Anne Beech of Pluto Press for her painstaking efforts.

Preface

This book is neither a textbook nor a colouring book. The reader will not find a balanced overview and commentary on theories of consumption. Neither will the reader find any attempt to represent accurately all of the ideas of those theorists who are normally viewed as influential in theorising consumption. Such books exist in abundance. So much for what this book is not.

This book radically opposes what has become the dominant and most widely publicised theory of consumption around today. This theory is most commonly referred to as 'culturalist' theory. Its natural home is the academic field of Cultural Studies. The culturalist approach to consumption is so-called because it locates both the description and explanation of consumption in the interactions between consumer culture and the individual. This might, in the first instance, seem to be a reasonable starting place for theorising consumption. But things are not what they seem.

First, 'consumer culture' is defined in ways that more or less exclude its essential characteristics. Much is written about the *images* of consumer culture produced by advertising, shopping malls, theme parks and the mass media. Very little is written about consumer culture as an economic phenomenon. Second, this incredible omission extends to an explanation of individual consumption. We might suppose that our capacity to consume is based on the money we have at our disposal. Not so for culturalist theory.

No-nonsense consumers might suppose that they need money to buy *goods* and *services*, and that they make their purchases maybe for practical reasons, perhaps to satisfy needs. Forget it. Culturalist theory has it that what we actually consume are images, meanings, symbolic values, dreams, fantasies and the like. Money does not come into the reckoning for the simple reason that all of these non-material things come free.

Third, consumer *culture*, for culturalist theory, is not so much the product of commercial interests, as the ongoing, dynamic, continuously re-made outcome of individuals' interactions with it. Consumer culture is, if you like, in substantial part, the product of imaginative, creative and playful consumers. Portrayed as such, consumer culture is wholly positive. It is 'meaningful' and our participation in it promises to enrich our lives. It is so meaningful that it has become *the site* in which we become who we are and choose who we want to be. I consume, therefore I am.

Fourth, consumer culture is not only all-pervasive; in the hands of culturalist theory, it is just about all that there is. All that might be called 'culture' or 'cultural' is contained within consumer culture. We live in a consumer culture. Now, again this might appear to be reasonable, but given the narrow way in which consumer culture is defined by culturalist theory, it is anything but reasonable. Needless to say the consumer culture depicted by Cultural Studies is something other than the consumer culture that is differently experienced by different people. Yet culturalist theory claims to be based on the 'lived experience of ordinary people'!

I do not intend to provide, here, an account of the various ways consumer culture is experienced, but we could suppose that any theory claiming to be based on the lived experience of ordinary people would devote some attention to the material contradictions thrown up by consumer culture. Yet those academics who are intoxicated by the *powerful images* of consumer culture have nothing to say, for example, about the people with poverty-etched faces, clutching plastic bags, who seek shelter in glitzy shopping malls, only to find themselves forever 'moved on' by security guards.

One might suppose, too, that such a theory would tap into people's commonly voiced understandings and criticisms of consumer culture. But culturalist theory affords no space, for example, to widely shared suspicions that consumers are routinely 'ripped-off'. Perhaps Cultural Studies is afraid of pursuing this. It might, after all, lead into discussions of profit and capitalism, and this, given that Marxism is no longer trendy, would be a most unfashionable step to take. There is no need to be afraid. Consumers' perceptions of being ripped-off are not based on a Marxist analysis – they do not have to be. They derive, in the main, from the knowledge of differences, some of them huge, in the prices charged by different retailers for identical products, from the reported levels of profit achieved by major companies and financial institutions, and from the reported salaries and bonuses paid out to chief executive officers and senior managers.

Cultural Studies steers clear of anything that might disturb the world of fictions that it currently inhabits. It is no longer the study of culture. (To emphasise this I refer to 'Cultural Studies' rather than 'cultural studies'.) To those blessed with a fair measure of common-sense, the culturalist theory of consumption, an elaborate fiction like so many products of an academic world that is cut off from reality, can be ignored as an irrelevance. However, I have chosen not to, primarily because the cultural theory of consumption is politically important.

I am not referring here to the politics of identity, which, according to Cultural Studies, is played out in the arena of consumption. Today, this politics of identity is divorced from its emancipatory roots and has become a form of privatism – an apolitical self-absorption. Rather I am referring to how the cultural theory of consumption, whose main mouthpiece is the make-believe world of the mass media, contributes to a distorted perception of social reality that appears to be shared by some members of some governments. This is not surprising given the growing chasm between politicians and the people that they are supposed to represent.

The fictions of the culturalist theory of consumption contribute to a number of myths: the myth of widespread affluence, the myth that everybody is gripped by the motive to consume more and more, and the myth that everybody finds the attractions of consumerism irres-istible. The culturalist theory of consumption also provides politicians with numerous ideas that can be used either to ignore, or to put a positive spin on, deprivation and social inequalities, to justify their promotion of big business, entrepeneurship, and forms of social and environmental impoverishment in the name of wealth creation. It is on the basis of such credentials that the culturalist theory of consumption, whatever the intentions of those who have influenced its development and those who perpetuate it, is best seen not as a theory dispassionately forged in the interests of truth, but as an *ideology* that can be used to legitimate the illegitimate directions pursued by big business.

For Anti-capitalists

Introduction

During the past ten years or so, within the academic fields of the sociology of culture and Cultural Studies, a theoretical consensus has emerged with respect to the study of consumption. This consensus portrays the realm of consumption as an arena of choice and individual freedom, it focuses on the meaningful nature of consumption – its symbolic value rather than its material use value, and it emphasises the significance of consumption for the formation, maintenance and expression of self-identity and lifestyle. Consumption is both described and explained within the theoretical framework provided by this consensus. This does not mean that consumption as a field of study is devoid of theoretical conflicts and debates, but it does mean that what debates and conflicts there are take place *within* the boundaries of the consensus. Alternative descriptions and explanations of consumption are ignored or dismissed as irrelevant (and are thus marginalised), or they are inappropriately squeezed into the interpretative framework of the consensus (and are thus misrepresented).

The purpose of this book is to demonstrate that the theoretical consensus I have identified above is fundamentally wrong. This is not to say that it contains no truth whatsoever. Like most ideologies it contains little, partial truths that are fielded as the whole truth. And, in doing so, the most significant truths are missing. As a consequence the description and explanation of consumption provided by the theoretical consensus is highly distorted and basically misleading. It is for this reason that I refer to the theoretical consensus as an *ideology,* specifically the most recent form of the ideology of consumerism. It should be clear that 'ideology' is being used here in its critical, perjorative sense.

The latest ideology of consumerism trades off a number of facts that cannot be denied – the increasing commercialisation and commodification of everyday life, the growing volume of commodities in circulation, and the fact that almost everybody, at least in the advanced capitalist societies, addresses their *needs and wants* by purchasing goods, services and experiences rather than providing these for themselves. I have highlighted 'needs and wants' because

1

the failure to distinguish basic needs from wants, and more specifically from preferences, is, in my view, the basis for the recent development of the ideology of consumerism, that is, the basis of most of the distortions inherent in this ideology. This failure, too, plays a significant part in the loss of the distinction between consumption and consumerism. The growing tendency is to use these concepts interchangeably. It will be important for the arguments developed throughout this book, for explanatory and political reasons, that consumerism is not conflated with consumption. For the moment I will merely assert that consumption refers to all that is consumed. Consumerism, as I use the term, refers to consumption that is not intended to address needs (unnecessary consumption) and consumption that adresses needs but in unnecessarily superfluous forms. I acknowledge that my distinction between consumption and consumerism has been made problematic by the incorporation of the superfluous within basic necessities. However my distinction is not intended to be precise – it cannot be. It is made in recognition of the fact that the primary purpose of a proportion of consumption is intended to address survival needs.

There are reasons for the ideology of consumerism's failure to distinguish needs from wants or preferences. At first glance these reasons might appear to be sound enough. They tend to stem from an emphasis on the relative nature of needs. Much is made of the notion that needs are not given, fixed or absolute, but are culturally defined. In other words what constitutes a need varies from society to society, from culture to culture, group to group, etc. And the same variation exists with regard to what constitutes the satisfaction of needs.

A logical extension of this argument has it that in the final analysis, what constitutes a need is relative to the individual. In other words needs vary from individual to individual, as does their satisfaction. One individual's need can be another person's want and vice versa. Furthermore, it is argued, it is only the individual who is in a position to determine his or her own needs and wants and how they are to be satisfied. Besides, it is maintained, given that consumers have to make choices with regard to the satisfaction of their needs and wants, does it make any practical difference whether or not their preferences reflect needs or wants?[1]

The objection that this kind of reasoning adopts a loose concept of need and fails to account for the 'special' status of basic needs is brushed aside by the ideology of consumerism. Within the thinking of cultural relativism basic needs have the same status as all needs.

On top of this it can be argued that when it comes to actual consumption the goods that are purchased, including those goods that might count as basic necessities, increasingly embody cultural meanings or symbolic values. Further, there may be little or no difference amongst comparable commodities, including basic necessities, in terms of purchase price, utility and, where relevant, durability. But differences between comparable goods do exist in terms of their symbolic value. It is thus concluded that the preferences of individual consumers are best understood as reflecting symbolic values rather than use values.

The description of all consumption as primarily symbolic, that is as an expression of culturally-based meaning and motivated by the search for meaning, does key in rather neatly with the ideology of consumerism's emphasis on the pivotal significance of consumption for self-identity (meanings attributed by the self to itself) formation. It also consolidates the ideology's portrayal of the realm of consumption as a realm of freedom. This manifests itself not only in the assumption that what is consumed reflects the preferences or choices of the individual, but also in the assumption that these preferences arise from motivations rooted in symbolic (post-necessity) values. Post-necessity consumption summons up images of freedom, and in equating freedom with affluence post-necessity values are identified exclusively with consumerism.

Under the universalising tendencies of the ideology of consumerism – *all* consumers have to make choices (a forced freedom); *all* consumption is symbolic; *all* consumption involves self-identity – we are provided with an image of high consuming societies that contradicts the experience of the majority. I do concede that the ideology of consumerism may reflect the experience of *minorities*. Needless to say, it cannot be assumed that what is true for a few small groups is applicable to all. I shall argue that basic needs, as sources of consumer motivations, continue to be highly relevant, even in the so-called affluent societies.

This is not to say that all consumption is reducible to the satisfaction of basic needs – it clearly is not. However, the relevance of basic needs for an explanation of consumption resides *in the consequences of the alienation of labour, and the consequences of employment for our total range of action.* Quite simply the alienation of labour (we no longer directly produce for our own needs) means that we are *forced* to satisfy basic needs by purchasing the relevant goods, and income from employment is what enables most people in the more affluent societies to satisfy survival needs. But being employed also structures our time and affects our energies. I shall argue that the effects of employment, for a majority, are such that the range of action and scope for autonomous action are severely restricted. Consumption (including unnecessary consumption) is one type of activity that is served by, fits in with, and reinforces these restrictions. In a sense an important factor in the explanation of consumption is the recognition that it arises in circumstances in which individuals are resourced for very little else.

To argue this, the main focus of Part Two, is to argue against the ideology of consumerism's emphasis on consumption as a realm in which individuals are freely motivated to pursue post-necessity values. This is not to deny the significance of post-necessity values. Indeed I shall argue on the back of empirical evidence, that the post-necessity values which seem to be most widely shared, even amongst the poor, can be best served only in ways other than consumption.

As I have already noted, the ideology of consumerism transforms the description and explanation of consumption intended (motivated) to address basic needs into a free expression (choice) of symbolic values. This will not do. What is lost here is the continuing relevance of basic needs for an explanation of consumption. We can acknowledge that basic needs are open to culturally-loaded interpretations and can be satisfied in culturally diverse ways. But this does not mean that basic needs are irrelevant. They are certainly not irrelevant to the vast majority. The latter are not only able to distinguish basic needs from wants, they consistently attribute more importance to basic needs than to wants. The deprivation of basic needs, for example, is widely treated as a far more serious matter than unsatisfied wants, and is almost universally regarded as intolerable by virtue of the harm caused to human beings. We cannot say the same about the deprivation of wants.

Underpinning this difference between needs and wants is the recognition that there are universal needs relevant to an individual's survival and well-being, whereas wants tend to be associated with the mere preferences of particular individuals. Likewise, as sources of our motives, basic needs are altogether more substantial, more enduring, and generally, if not always, more powerful than wants. A theory of consumption that ignores the significant role of basic needs as a source of consumer motivation is itself largely irrelevant – irrelevant to the experiences of the vast majority, even the vast majority in the advanced capitalist societies.

In ignoring basic needs the ideology of consumerism promotes a view of the individual as somewhat more superficial than is actually the case. This distortion, as we shall see in Part One, manifests itself in the ideology of consumerism's treatment of each of its elements. In its treatment of consumption as symbolic or reflecting post-necessity values, in addition to ignoring the material use value of what is consumed, relatively superficial meanings are foregrounded to the neglect of *the meaningful*. In its treatment of identity, it ignores the fact that there are many sources of self-identity other than commodities, it ignores identity-needs and re-defines identity as image and style. And in its treatment of consumption as a realm of freedom, it ignores the fact that our actual freedom is limited by the alienation of labour and the organisation of employment, and it embraces a concept of free action that is little more than inconsequential multiple-choice activity.

The failure to acknowledge the effects of the alienation of labour and the impact of employment on income, time and physical and mental energy on our range of action does radically undermine the explanatory power of the ideology of consumerism. The ideology of consumerism has developed in an academic context (primarily Cultural Studies) in which there has been a concerted effort to avoid explaining cultural practices in economic terms. Whatever the merits of avoiding economistic accounts of cultural matters, there is clearly a danger of bypassing the relevance of economic power where it is, to ordinary mortals, most relevant. To attempt to explain consumption without any reference to economic power, which is what the ideology of consumerism does, is sheer folly. Instead, the culture-centredness behind the ideology of consumerism trains its attention on the interactions between consumer culture and the individual.

In attempting to locate the sources of the reasons and motivations for individual consumption in the interactions between consumer culture and the individual without considering the economic (and other) preconditions of consumption, the ideology of consumerism does not explain consumption at all. Instead we get speculative psychocentric (meaning, pleasure, self-identity) accounts of the interactions between consumer culture and the individual, which are fielded as explanations of consumption. Speculations about how commodified meanings are subverted by individuals in their quest for a certain image or style may help to explain an individual's preference for a Peugeot, for example, over other brands of cars, but it does not explain why an individual buys a car in the first place, or prefers a car to a bicycle as a primary means of private transport. In elevating psychocentric speculations to the status of explanation, the ideology of consumerism runs the risk of attributing motives and reasons to individuals that either do not exist or are of little significance, while simultaneously ignoring what is most relevant to the vast majority.

Restoring needs to a central role in the explanation of consumption is not intended to restore a little balance to the orthodox theoretical consensus. It is intended to *replace* this orthodoxy by initiating an explanation of consumption that is rooted in the experience of the majority. This, I believe, is necessary for the simple reason that the latest ideology of consumerism is influential beyond the academic world – not amongst consumers, but with big business, governments, the mass media and even amongst those who are justifiably critical of consumerism.

The practical manifestation of the ideology of consumerism is, as it has always been, most clearly seen in the marketing strategies and advertising techniques used by big business. This is no surprise. Big business, after all, is solely about making profits, and the consumer is an obvious source of profit. It is also no surprise that the ideology of consumerism is actively promoted by the mass media. The mass media are big business in their own right and are vital to all business in so far as they are primarily concerned with selling audiences to advertisers.

In their elaboration of the ideology of consumerism academics provide a convenient justification, should producers ever need it, for the wasteful and polluting production of goods. Producers are increasingly in the habit of informing us that 'we produce only those goods that people tell us they want. And, we know that we are giving people what they want because they are buying our products.' Such is the thinking behind the idea that consumption is increasingly 'consumer-led'. In the meantime wasteful production (wasteful in terms of energy and resources, including labour-time, and in terms of polluting waste) continues – not because the consumer has demanded it but because of the profits to be made.

Whether or not governments are persuaded that consumption is consumer-led is another issue. We do know, however, that governments in their acquiescing subordination to big business are unlikely to get in the way of wasteful production. The influence of the ideology of consumerism on governments, however, does take other forms. The images of affluence generated by the ideology of consumerism enable governments to over-estimate the degree and level of affluence in their societies, and the extent to which insubstantial consumer motivations have become dominant. These errors (mis)inform a whole range of government policies, from taxation to welfare, and it is through the consequences of economic and social policies that individuals experience the ideology of consumerism in a significant way.

It is just these errors, too, that infiltrate the thinking of many anti-capitalists and Greens who are critical of consumerism. Escalating levels of consumption are too readily assumed to reflect the growing affluence of *individuals*. This assumption needs to be contested. Sure enough individuals do consume, but so too do *institutions*. What I refer to as institutional consumption, and its significance for wasteful production, will be discussed in Part Three. It is here that the anti-capitalist and Green social policy implications of my central arguments will be briefly noted.

Until the latest development in the ideology of consumerism, a critical distance between academic theories of consumption and the promotion of consumption could be clearly observed. This is no longer the case. In an earlier era the false claims and clever manip-ulations of advertisers were easy meat for academic critics. When goods were promoted in terms of the superior use value of ready-made products over self-produced goods, academic critics bemoaned the undermining of self-reliance and traditional ways of life. When the promotional emphasis developed into the value of consumption for the achievement of social status and for the prevention of the loss of status (keeping up with the Joneses) academic critics were quick to point out that the competitive individualism of consumer culture was replacing the value of co-operation, and with it, social solidarity and community spirit. Underpinning much of the academic criticism in the past was the view that the promotion of consumer products was essentially about getting people to consume things that they did not really need. Today, the theoretical consensus, in attempting to explain consumption without reference to need, has lost the most significant basis there is for a critique of consumerism. How the dominant academic theory of consumption has come to coincide with the promotion of consumerism will be the focus of the first chapter.

Part One

The Ideology of Consumerism

1 The Latest Ideology of Consumerism

The dominant theory of consumption, at least within Cultural Studies and the sociology of culture,[1] provides a highly positive assessment of consumerism. As I suggested in the Introduction this assessment is based on a description and explanation of consumption that is fundamentally wrong – it is both conceptually muddled and empirically under-informed. The purpose of this chapter is to begin to explain how this has come about. To put it a little more pointedly: how have fields that were once highly critical of consumerism come to embrace it, celebrate it and promote it?

In attempting to answer this question I will begin by reproducing in outline what is often routinely trotted out as the starting place for the development of the current consensus on consumption. In a widely used undergraduate text it is made patently clear that traditional, critical theories of consumption are no longer adequate. We are told that 'The traditional view is demonstrated *par excellence* in the perspective known as the "mass culture critique", or "the production of consumption perspective".'[2]

The Frankfurt School, as all students of Cultural Studies and the sociology of culture are repeatedly informed, are identified as the key theorists of the production of consumption perspective. The author then proceeds to offer the standard interpretation of this theory. We are told that the Frankfurt School

argued that the expansion of mass production in the twentieth century had led to the commodification of culture, with the rise of culture industries. Consumption served the interests of manufacturers seeking greater profits, and citizens became the passive victims of advertisers. Processes of standardization, they argued, were accompanied by the development of a materialistic culture, in which commodities came to lack authenticity and instead merely met 'false' needs. These needs were generated by marketing and advertising strategies and, it is argued, increased the capacity for ideological control or domination.[3]

The author goes on to note how the production of consumption perspective embodied arguments 'containing ... a strong undercurrent of moral outrage about change and, especially, about conspicuous and excessive consumption'. He then repeats a point made earlier about arguments concerning the 'rise of leisure and consumption activities' increasing 'the capacity for ideological control and domination', and detracting 'from more "authentic" experience and from meeting human needs'. The growth of consumerism, he adds, 'is often associated with a decline in collective activity and in the public sphere, and the growing privatization (in the home) of our daily lives'.[4]

I will address this misreading of the Frankfurt School early in Chapter 5. For my purposes here, however, I am not in the least bit concerned about this one-sided interpretation, and thus misrepresentation of the Frankfurt School's treatment of consumption. The important point is that this interpretation is a standard one, and it conveniently sets up (as its antithesis) the 'obviously reasonable' current thinking about consumption. Thus in concluding the brief summary of the production of consumption perspective, the author states that 'Crucially, this perspective attributed to consumers a profoundly passive role, portraying them as manipulated, mindless dupes, rather than as active creative beings.'[5]

Here we begin to get a flavour of the current theoretical orthodoxy – a theory that avoids depictions of the individual consumer as passive, manipulated and mindless. It is rather a theory that embraces the view that the individual consumer is active and creative, and by extension, *free*. Our textbook positively draws on 'subcultural' studies of young consumers to indicate how this freedom is used.

> Rather than being passive and easily manipulated, they [researchers] found that young consumers were active, creative and critical in their appropriation and transformation of material artefacts. In a process of *bricolage,* they appropriated, re-accented, rearticulated or trans-coded the material of mass culture to their own ends, through a range of everyday creative and symbolic practices. Through such processes of appropriation, identities are constructed.[6]

In a nutshell the emphases of the latest ideology of consumerism on freedom, identity and the symbolic nature of consumption are given explicit expression.

The distance between the interpretation of the critical theory of the Frankfurt School and the current theoretical orthodoxy on consumption has been filled by numerous theoretical twists and turns. For the remainder of this chapter I shall try to avoid following each twist and turn. Rather I shall attempt to take the straightest possible line in unravelling the development of today's theoretical consensus on consumption. This will inevitably mean that I cannot do justice to the details and subtleties of all the theoretical debates that provide a backdrop to current thinking about consumption. But hopefully my analysis will enable those outside of Cultural Studies to begin to understand what, on the face of it, might appear to be incomprehensible.

It is with the outsider in mind that I will occasionally raise a few obvious criticisms of the latest theoretical orthodoxy. But for the most part I shall save my criticisms for later chapters. Neither is my task that of providing a fair representation of the academic fields of Cultural Studies and the sociology of culture. Rather, I am primarily concerned with explaining the emergence of the latest ideology of consumerism. This will entail a discussion of enduring tendencies within Cultural Studies that predispose this field to be receptive to certain elements of postmodern theory that have been particularly influential in shaping the positive portrayal of consumption.

Cultural Studies

The latest ideology of consumerism can be understood in the context of the history of Cultural Studies. I do not intend to provide a detailed history of Cultural Studies; this has been done elsewhere.[7] However, I will focus on a number of underlying tendencies that have been in place throughout the brief history of this field.[8] These tendencies, I shall go on to argue, have provided a receptive ground for a number of theoretical currents, both within and outside of Cultural Studies, that have been influential in transforming the study of consumption. The underlying tendencies of Cultural Studies that strike me as being most relevant to the latest ideology of consumerism are: the textualisation of everything, ideology-centredness and anti-elitism.

The Textualisation of Everything

Today 'culture' is a term that is used in a variety of ways. It can refer to a way of life that is lived by particular groups, to discernible values embodied in particular activities, for example, club culture, drug culture, football culture, or to particular values that permeate certain institutions or even the whole society, for example, canteen culture, racist culture, and so on. 'Culture' is still used in some quarters to refer solely to activities relevant to the production and consumption of cultural products such as novels, films, music and so on. All of these usages of 'culture' have figured in Cultural Studies. However, it is fair to say that Cultural Studies has been increasingly dominated by a concern with cultural products that are deemed to be popular in some way.

Some popular cultural products come in the form of actual texts, for example magazines, or, as in the case of television programmes, can be readily studied as actual texts. In studying texts Cultural Studies has been gradually taken with the idea that any given text is open to a limitless range of interpretations. Thus while texts are full of meaning (meaningful), the meanings which the reader or viewer brings to the text will strongly influence the meaning made from the text. Now, the realisation that this kind of (meaningful) inter-action can take place (many might argue that it does take place) between individuals and the *non-textual*, has enabled Cultural Studies to treat *anything and everything as a text*, that is, as something that is full of potential meaning. It is on this basis that theory unproblematically transforms all objects of consumption into texts. As we shall see, this sets up the description of consumption as an activity in which we consume signs in order to create or play with meaning.

I do not dispute that objects of consumption can be said to have a 'sign value' or symbolic value and that consuming things may involve the consumer in a creative play with meaning, and may for this or other reasons be pleasurable. What I do dispute is the appropriateness of treating all that we consume as texts that are full of potential meaning. Might it not be the case that the very process of textualisation encourages an over-reading of much that we consume? How relevant is a description of consumption as an act involving a play with meaning for most consumers? Do most individuals consume in order to participate in symbolic play? Do most consumers consume signs, first and foremost, rather than objects? For whom is consuming signs or playing with meaning meaningful?

The textualisation of everything, while it opens up everything for endless interpretation, does also lead to an inappropriate and restrictive account of consumption, and one that more often than not misses the point. When the consumption of food, for example, is treated solely as a symbolic activity, the main purpose of consuming food does not figure in its explanation.

Ideology-centredness

The tendency of Cultural Studies to textualise everything, and thus to focus on meanings, is consistent with its emphasis on ideology. In many respects the study of culture, whatever it has been taken to mean, has been and still is the study of ideologies – 'ideology' broadly understood as an organised set of meanings usually, but not always, supportive of the interests of particular groups. An ideology is typically viewed to be more substantial, more powerful and more socially significant than random or scattered meanings. Cultural Studies, at least in Britain, arose in part out of the concern of the New Left to articulate the relations between capitalist economy, capitalist state and culture in ways that avoided a crude economic reductionism. This articulation was theorised almost exclusively in terms of theories of ideology.

In avoiding economic reductionism Cultural Studies had difficulties in addressing the question of economic determinism. Rather than explore the obvious power of capital in shaping the mass media and the educational system, two of the most important agencies of mass culture and ideological transmission, the economic was declared 'to determine in the last instance', and that was that! Ideological power could be studied without reference to the economic, as if it (ideology) operated relatively autonomously. In a sense ideological power was given the same status as the power of the economy and the state – the economic base no longer determined the superstructure, and the forces of reproduction were deemed to be as powerful as the forces of production. As we shall see later, in elevating the power of ideology and ignoring economic determinants, Cultural Studies was free to study consumption as a practice divorced from commercial manipulations.

In the early days of Cultural Studies, and into the 1980s, ideology-critique was at the forefront of its concerns. The dominant ideology, in its various manifestations, was subjected to incisive, critical analysis. This work was viewed as politically significant in so far as it was widely assumed that the reproduction of the advanced capitalist societies was dependent on the effective manipulations of the dominant ideology on the public. This assumption, central to what is known as *the dominant ideology thesis,* framed the whole field of Cultural Studies. As challenges to this assumption, primarily from social and political theorists, gained momentum, Cultural Studies stuck to its guns – its ideology-centredness. Cultural Studies academics believed in the dominant ideology thesis. The 'popularity' of Thatcherism, many argued, was living proof of the validity of the dominant ideology thesis.

Criticism of the dominant ideology thesis came from a range of theoretical positions. There were those who maintained that ideological power was insignificant in relation to economic and state power in controlling people.[9] Some backed up this view by noting the lack of empirical support for the effectiveness of the dominant ideology on the subordinate.[10] While these critics of the dominant ideology thesis may not have done justice to the re-working of this thesis via the use of hegemony theory, they nevertheless agreed with the advocates of the thesis that a dominant ideology exists. However, there were (and still are) critics of the dominant ideology thesis who maintain that a dominant ideology no longer exists. This view, which was originally associated with right-wing academics known as 'liberal-pluralists', was given a vigorous airing by postmodernists. The latter, in their attack on *all* grand narratives, theoretically swept away the grand narrative of the dominant ideology.

Postmodern discourses, at least from the late 1980s, began to exert an influence on Cultural Studies. Cultural Studies drifted away from its critique of the dominant ideology, and gradually gave up the dominant ideology thesis altogether. It embraced the postmodern view that there are a range of competing ideologies and that individuals use these selectively to make sense (meaning) of their own lives and to organise their actions. That our actions are governed by beliefs/values/meanings is a core assumption of the dominant ideology thesis. It remains a central tenet of much postmodernist theory. For Cultural Studies, ironically, it means the retention of the assumption that ideologies are powerful, but the ideologies in question are denuded of the social and political significance attributed to the dominant ideology.

Needless to say ideologies, like meanings, can be read as discourses or texts materialised in all consumer products. The latter, under the ideology-centredness of Cultural Studies, can be analysed as 'ideological' (irrespective of their reception) thereby adding an unwarranted seriousness and importance to the analysis. It must be said that not all Cultural Studies academics adopt a concept of ideology as merely an organised set of meanings cut off from any notion of the dominant. The latter remains important to some, and enables them to treat consumption as an arena of 'ideological struggle', in which the ideologies of a 'dominant order', or commodified meanings can be challenged.

Anti-elitism

Cultural Studies is renowned for its intended anti-elitism, or as some might put it, its populism. The anti-elitism of Cultural Studies initially manifested itself in at least four ways. First, there was an attempt to 'recover' working-class culture and promote its literary products in the face of a growing commercially driven mass culture. Second, while critical of mass culture, Cultural Studies nevertheless was just as critical of the critique of mass culture advanced by Theodor Adorno and Max Horkheimer. Adorno and Horkheimer were criticised for their alleged economic reductionism, their denigration of mass (popular) culture in relation to elite culture, and, as noted earlier, for their alleged disparaging view of the masses as being ideologically manipulated and duped by advertising and the products of mass culture. Third, 'deviant' and minority sub-cultures were studied from within these groups, and their stereotypical misrepresentation was shown to be a product of dominant, mainstream values (the dominant ideology). The latter were associated with elite culture. Finally, elite culture was, amongst other things, male and white. Cultural Studies opened up spaces for women and non-whites 'to speak for themselves'.

However, the anti-elitism of Cultural Studies gained momentum from a number of developments that I have already briefly discussed. In their early advocacy of the dominant ideology thesis Cultural Studies academics sought a way of theorising the effects of ideology on individuals that allowed some scope for different subjective responses. (It was wrongly assumed that Adorno and Horkheimer allowed no scope for this.) Instead, Cultural Studies turned to the theories of Louis Althusser and Antonio Gramsci.[11] Oddly enough Althusser's writings, particularly in conjunction with the psychoanalytic work of Jacques Lacan,[12] are far more deterministic than anything Adorno and Horkheimer ever produced. However, they were used to read the products of mass culture in terms of ideological 'subject-positions' on offer to audiences. What is important here is that very serious theory was applied to popular culture – a further step in legitimating the academic study of popular culture and raising its status in relation to elite or highbrow culture.

The turn to Gramsci proved to be far more useful in giving vent to the anti-elitist impulses of Cultural Studies. Gramsci's approach to the dominant ideology did allow room for its impact on individuals to be mediated by the individual's own common sense. The effects of the dominant ideology were 'negotiated', albeit within its broad framework. This idea was later to be divorced from the Gramscian project and developed on its own, as we have already seen, in the emphasis in Cultural Studies on consumption as a practice involving the active play of symbolic meaning.

Crucially, the influence of the cultural and epistemological relativism of postmodernism radicalised the value of interpretive freedom over and above attempts at objective judgement. In postmodern theory, any interpretation is as valid as any other. Anti-elitism can live forever. It matters not that many of the products of popular culture are trivial and intended to appeal to the lowest common denominator. The individual adopts a creatively playful stance toward them, makes meaning in using them, and in these ways may derive pleasure from them. Further, this applies equally to textual and non-textual products (that are nevertheless textualised).

Popular cultural products are by definition anti-elitist, but now (as opposed to the period during which Cultural Studies operated under the spell of the dominant ideology thesis) the ordinary person can be trusted to resist and subvert the ideologies carried in these products. In a major sense Cultural Studies, in its uncritical stance toward the products of popular culture, is attempting to divest itself of any traces of elitism. The popular, after all, is popular, it is assumed, because ordinary people have made it so. Criticism of the popular is too readily seen as also a criticism of ordinary people and this, in turn, is too readily seen as elitist.

Of course, crude definitions of 'the popular' may, on examination, reveal that the so-called popular is not as popular after all. Does winning a General Election with less than a third of the vote of the total electorate mean that the winner is popular? Is television popular because the amount of time the adult population spends in front of the box averages out at about 20 hours per week? Do people who spend in excess of 20 hours per week watching television actually do so for reasons attributed to them by Cultural Studies academics? Is there not an element (the patronising element) of elitism involved in celebrating as popular what most ordinary people know to be rubbish?

Anti-elitism need not necessarily develop into a celebration of 'the popular', but in pursuing this trajectory, anti-elitism dovetails rather neatly with the direction taken by the two other tendencies of Cultural Studies: ideology-centredness and the textualisation of everything. Indeed, these three tendencies interact with and reinforce each other, and provide the theoretical scaffolding for the latest ideology of consumerism. The foundations for approaching consumption as a symbolic activity are firmly in place. We have also seen that Cultural Studies is well disposed toward treating consumption as a realm of freedom – in its opposition to deterministic accounts of the individual, and in its assumption that the freedom of the consumer is unproblematically derived from interpretative freedom. All of these ideas will prove to be useful in the Cultural Studies treatment of consumption as a basis for identity formation.

However, theorising consumption as a realm of freedom and for its identity value took off in a big way as a consequence of ideas that surfaced outside of Cultural Studies. Nevertheless Cultural Studies has provided a receptive ground for these ideas and has proceeded to develop them in shaping the latest ideology of consumerism. I shall briefly discuss a number of the more important of these ideas below.

New Times

During the 1980s many social theorists were of the view that the advanced capitalist societies had (and were still) undergoing significant changes – changes in production technology, the growth of information technology, the expansion of electronic media, the development of global communication networks, the decline of heavy industries, the growth of service industries, the changing skill requirements of work, the erosion of communities, detraditionalisation, changing gender roles and so on. While the theorisation of these changes took radically different forms, I shall focus here on those ideas that quickly became mainstream in both the sociology of culture and Cultural Studies.

Particularly influential was the idea that the advanced capitalist societies had entered a new phase in their development. This new phase has attracted a variety of labels – new times, consumer capitalism, people's capitalism, late modernity, postmodernity. The *alleged* changes that constitute the new phase, however we label it, that strike me as being most relevant to the development of the latest ideology of consumerism are: the shift from Fordist to post-Fordist forms of production; the shift from a life-focus centred on work to one centred on consumption; the replacement of 'fixed' identities with fluid, consumption-based identities; and the de-materialisation of consumption.

I refer to these changes as 'alleged changes' in order to emphasise their contestable nature and that they derive from theories rather than facts. Indeed, the alleged changes are so closely interwoven with theoretical fashion that it will also be necessary to comment on the theoretical fashion that has been most influential in shaping the ideology of consumerism, namely postmodern theory. First, however, there will be a brief discussion of each of the alleged changes that I have identified above.

Post-Fordism?

Fordism is associated with the mass production of standardised goods for consumption by 'the masses'. Post-Fordism, by way of contrast, is associated with small-scale units of production producing non-standardised goods tailored to the tastes of particular groups of consumers: niche markets, market segments, targeted markets and so forth. The shift to post-Fordism, it is widely acknowledged, has come about as a consequence of technological innovations, particularly the micro-chip, in the productive process and in communications. Marketing professionals tell us that detailed market research can be readily incorporated into differential product design, suggesting that production is driven by consumer-derived information.

Needless to say, post-Fordism is portrayed as consumer-friendly. Frank Mort confirms this when he states that 'Advertisers and marketers are not simply the slaves of capital. They are the intermediaries who construct a dialogue between the market on the one hand and consumer culture on the other.' But, importantly for the ideology of consumerism, 'Product design and innovation, pricing and promotion, are shaped by the noises coming from the street.'[13] In other words, production is consumer-led. This means that Cultural Studies can go along with the significance of post-Fordism (an economic phenomenon) for shaping consumer culture without fear of being accused of economic reductionism. The economics of post-Fordism, after all, are consumer-determined! And, because this is assumed to be so, consumer products today are viewed as more likely to provide pleasure and meaning than was the case in the era of standardised production. Furthermore, consumption, it is assumed, has now become an arena of empowerment, an arena in which we are encouraged to express freely our desires. Fordism could never accommodate this – it was far too inflexible. While it was relevant to be critical of mass production, and the devious attempts of advertisers to foist their products on to ordinary people, consumer-led post-Fordism has removed the need to approach consumption critically. Marketing now bows to consumer sovereignty.

Cultural Studies, as we have seen, was already well disposed toward the notion of consumer sovereignty. The freedom of the consumer implied in the notion of consumer sovereignty is compatible with the aversion of Cultural Studies to elitist portrayals of the ordinary person as a manipulated dope. Throughout the 1980s, when the propaganda promoting consumer sovereignty was at its height, Cultural Studies wanted to develop a theory of the subject that allowed scope for human agency (and thus freedom) but also wanted to distance itself from the New Right's vigorous advocacy of the idea that individual freedom could be realised *only* in free market capitalism. However, the reluctance to embrace free market ideology was short-lived.

Anti-elitism and the increasing acceptance of the universality of interpretative freedom had already steered Cultural Studies into an uncritical stance toward popular cultural products. Now, influential voices outside of the New Right's propaganda machine were confirming the success of free market ideology – consumption, in all its forms, had indeed become *the* arena in which sovereign individuals express their freedom.

Consumption as Life-focus

Whatever post-Fordism means for consumption it has generated radical changes in work and working conditions. These changes have been, and still are, the focus of a growing, highly critical, literature. Cultural Studies has largely ignored this literature. There are reasons for this that I shall discuss in later chapters. At this point I merely want to note that the most scathing critiques of work and working conditions are rooted in a commitment to individual and collective autonomy conceptualised in ways that bear no relation to what 'consumer autonomy' has come to mean.[14] To draw on this critique would undermine the substance of the positive portrayals of consumption embodied in the latest ideology of consumerism.

Rather than follow this self-destructive path (self-destructive for the ideology of consumerism) Cultural Studies has been content to accept the view that the attractions of consumerism are now sufficiently powerful for consumption to have replaced work as the central focus of life. In the words of Zygmunt Bauman:

> ... consumer conduct (consumer freedom geared to the consumer market) moves steadily into the position of, simultaneously, the cognitive and moral focus of life, the integrative bond of the society, and the focus of systemic management. In other words, it moves into the selfsame position which in the past – during the 'modern' phase of capitalist society – was occupied by work in the form of wage labour. This means that in our time individuals are engaged (morally by society, functionally by the social system) first and foremost as consumers rather than as producers.[15]

Significantly for Cultural Studies, especially in the context of its anti-elitism, the freedoms and pleasures associated with consumerism cannot be dismissed as trivial. As today's life-focus they are of central importance to individuals and are thus not to be derided as insubstantial and of little consequence. But Bauman is also suggesting that consumption plays a pivotal role in the reproduction of capitalism. He makes this explicitly clear when he argues that

> The crucial task of soliciting behaviour functionally indispensable for the capitalist economic system, and at the same time harmless to the capitalist political system, may now be entrusted to the *consumer market* and its unquestionable attractions. Reproduction of the capitalist system is therefore achieved through individual freedom (in the form of consumer freedom, to be precise) ...[16]

Before the anti-elitism of Cultural Studies developed into an uncritical populism, Bauman's argument would have attracted some attention, if only because it is a contemporary alternative to the dominant ideology thesis. But Cultural Studies is no longer interested in explaining the reproduction of capitalism. This is significant in so far as understanding how the system is reproduced is essential in formulating effective opposition to capitalism. In disconnecting consumption as a life-focus from its role in the reproduction of capitalism, and devoting all of its attention to the former, Cultural Studies has effectively divorced itself from its radical roots.

Identity

To accept that the transition from Fordism to post-Fordism has resulted in consumption replacing work as the life-focus of individuals is also to accept that consumption has replaced work as the basis of individual identities. While it is true that identities are rooted in ways of life, and can thus be expected to change when established ways of life change or disappear altogether, Cultural Studies has unproblematically accepted a narrow view of this process.

Quite simply it is generally agreed that people's sense of who they are was, in earlier times, fairly fixed in terms of a secure job, a stable community spanning several generations and a relatively stable family. Children were socialised to follow in their parents' footsteps, eventually taking on prescribed adult roles that obeyed traditional gender divisions – the life-focus for males was employment and for females domestic labour. With the decline of heavy industries, the growth of new industries and the service sector, jobs were relocated, work changed, communities disintegrated and family ties were stretched and loosened. At the same time traditions were challenged as individuals had to forge new ways of living. As a consequence people found themselves uprooted from what had been the secure foundations of their identities.

It might be assumed that amongst those individuals most affected by these changes there would be some who would experience distress. While there is some acknowledgement of this, Cultural Studies has been more inclined to adopt the view that people were *liberated* from traditions and narrow role prescriptions. The changes opened up a whole world of consumption that is far more exciting and pleasurable than the drudgery of work. To be sure people still have to work, but now do not have to restrict their life-focus to work alone. Of course, there are clear signs that a majority of people do not identify themselves with their work, but it is a massive assumption to make that *the* alternative to work is consumption. Cultural Studies makes this assumption and proceeds to theorise contemporary identities solely in terms of what people consume.

Essentially, Cultural Studies wholeheartedly adopts the view that in consuming we consume signs or meanings. Some go on to emphasise that the meanings arise from the relational position of goods to each other within a system or code, and it is these meanings that determine our identities when we consume. However, by far the most popular view has it that individuals, rather than signs, are the meaning-makers, and the most important meanings are those we attribute to ourselves (self-identities). It is these meanings that are used to attribute meaning to what we consume, and the meaning consumed becomes part of our self-identities. In both views identity becomes an open-ended, fluid entity that is more or less continuously re-fashioned. But in the popular view it is the individual who actively assembles and reshapes his or her own identity through consumption.

So the upheavals promulgated by post-Fordist capitalism, far from plunging people into some kind of identity-crisis, are understood to have actually liberated individuals. People are no longer bound by restrictive, and in many cases oppressive and repressive, identities. Thanks to the proliferation of consumer goods, and thus consumer choices, people are now free to choose who they are and what they become. Seen in this way, consumption is obviously a good thing.

In arriving at this position, as I shall demonstrate in Chapter 3, Cultural Studies has exercised a tunnel vision created by its own internal structures. Not only does it ignore the continuing relevance of sources of identity other than from the self in interaction with consumer products, but it transforms the concept of identity into something other than it actually is – something less substantial, less enduring, more trivial and superficial, and thus less meaningful and important. In this light it will make little sense to portray consumption as the great liberator.

De-materialisation

The textualisation of everything, within Cultural Studies, was boosted in the 1980s by observations that the transition to post-Fordism brought with it an unprecedented de-materialisation of society. Not only was consumption increasingly de-materialised, but it was taking place in a de-materialised context – a context saturated with the fantasy-inspiring images of advertising, shopping malls adorned with aesthetic images and a context in which televisual imagery occupied increasing amounts of time and space. Texts, it seemed, were just as 'real' as reality. Consumer products, it was widely noted, increasingly incorporated aesthetic knowledge (commodity aesthetics) in their design, display and packaging. The textual was infusing the non-textual. Aesthetic, that is non-material, considerations, such as colour, shape and feel, that are irrelevant to the material use value of consumer objects, were becoming more prominent, and for Cultural Studies more important. It is just these kinds of non-material considerations that are uppermost in the images promoted by advertising. Sometimes this emphasis is so strong that advertisements make no reference to the product itself.

For Cultural Studies the de-materialisation of consumption confirms the validity of textualising everything. However, the theorisation of the consequences of de-materialisation by Jean Baudrillard went way beyond anything that seemed imaginable within Cultural Studies.[17] Baudrillard's writings were highly influential. Their boldness appeared to give Cultural Studies the confidence to theorise consumption as nothing other than a symbolic activity.

Prior to the influence of Baudrillard Cultural Studies, in its structuralist phase, had been drawn to the use of semiotic methodologies in the analyses of texts. In semiotics the meanings of texts are generated autonomously, from within the text, as a consequence of the differences between signs within a symbolic code. It is thus possible (and desirable) to analyse texts without recourse to referents beyond the text. However, what was a methodology in Cultural Studies, is, in the hands of Baudrillard, a generative social force. Quite simply, for Baudrillard, the transition to post-Fordism has resulted in a society that is dominated and organised by a system of signs. Further, consumption is first and foremost the consumption of signs. Material commodities have a sign value, and their actual sign value is generated (semiotically) from within the system of signs. Exchange value and use value are no longer relevant in consumption.

So there is no need to transform consumer products into texts methodologically – they *are* as signs the stuff of texts. In a massive speculative leap, consumption *is* de-materialised – it *is* a symbolic activity. This much, at least, Cultural Studies is more than happy to embrace, and it can do so without adopting the most extreme expressions of Baudrillard's thinking. However, while Baudrillard's influence went further than this, it is fair to say that the new ideology of consumerism was already set on a path that would steer it clear of some of the implications of Baudrillard's position.

In some respects criticisms of some of Baudrillard's formulations do highlight the particular shape taken by the ideology of consumerism. The power that Baudrillard attributes to the system of signs, many have argued, goes too far. For Baudrillard identities are essentially the product of signs that we consume. Such a notion is far too deterministic for the ideology of consumerism – it allows no scope for individuals freely choosing and actively constructing their identities through a creative appropriation of signs. Indeed, Baudrillard is highly critical of any notion supportive of the ideology of consumer freedom: 'the freedom and sovereignty of the consumer are mystification pure and simple'.[18]

Baudrillard is also critical of the society produced by the generative power of a system of signs – images have replaced substance. It is thus a depthless, superficial world devoid of meaning. This will not do for the ideology of consumerism. Not only does Baudrillard fail to allow any scope for individual freedom in consumption and identity formation, but the identities produced by the system of signs, in his scheme of things, must inevitably be superficial and meaningless. This clearly violates the populist foundations of the ideology of consumerism.

In opposition to Baudrillard, the dominant current in Cultural Studies is committed to the view that the symbolic value of what is consumed is far from superficial. Rather, it is pregnant with potential meaning which becomes actual meaning through the creative activity of the consumer.

Postmodern Theory

The transition from Fordism to post-Fordism is often described as the transition from modernity to postmodernity. Amongst the most often cited characteristics of postmodernity are: the centrality of consumption (a postmodern society is a consumer society), the increasing social prominence and significance of the individual and self-identity, the spreading de-materialisation or aestheticisation of everyday life and with it the growing ascendancy of the symbolic and cultural not just in relation to economic and state power, but in constituting these powers, and the relativisation of values.

Postmodern theory has contributed to the particular identification of recent social changes, discussed above. But, postmodern theory's relevance to the latest ideology of consumerism resides more in its specific (some might say 'peculiar') interpretation of these changes. While Cultural Studies and the sociology of culture accommodate a variety of theories, it is fair to say that the influence of postmodern discourses is dominant in these fields. These discourses are no longer, as some critics supposed, a fleeting academic fashion – they have generated ideas that have become a major part of what is taken for granted in theorising consumption. Additionally, while all ideas that are fielded as postmodern are not automatically taken on board, they can, as in the case of some of Baudrillard's excesses, stimulate the development of more credible ideas.

Those working within Cultural Studies and the sociology of culture may feel that I have overstated the influence of postmodern theory in shaping the current theoretical consensus on consumption. In my defence I have noted an unwillingness amongst those theorising consumption to go the whole way with the postmodern thrust. To do so would either stretch the credibility of the theoretical consensus, or would render it insignificant. Thus while the consensus portrays consumption as a symbolic activity, it is not prepared to assert that all we consume is signs. The consensus, however, is comfortable with the idea that symbolic values provide the main reasons for what we consume. The consensus, too, is not entirely at ease with the postmodern concept of the totally fluid identity fluctuating in a wild sea of signs. Such a view undermines the seriousness of identity, and thus any theory of consumption that promotes its own social significance on the basis of the identity value of consumption. It also trivialises the freedom implied in consumer choices and in the concept of consumer sovereignty.

However, the real influence of postmodern theory is not so much in the substantive content of its ideas, but more in their methodological application. Postmodern theory emphasises that postmodern times are characterised by 'the blurring of boundaries'. Common distinctions that were made in an earlier era are said to be disappearing or, in some cases, no longer exist. Examples include distinctions between capital and labour, capitalist class and working class, middle class and working class, male and female, culture and nature, mind and body, the embodied self and the disembodied self, inner self and outer self, the material and the symbolic, sign and referent, sign and reality, theory and fiction, truth and fiction, and so on almost endlessly. Needless to say there is a mass of literature that is not convinced that all boundaries have been blurred.[19]

Postmodern theory, however, does privilege the power of the sign (the symbolic), and the flattening of distinctions, where applicable, follows one direction, the de-materialising, de-substantialising direction that is motored by the profusion of signs. Cultural Studies does not have to accept the total de-materialisation of society as a fact, but it does give considerable credence to this notion. It is convenient to do so in order to elevate the importance of consumption as a de-materialised, symbolic activity.

The de-materialising direction pursued by postmodern thinking acts as a methodological principle, that is, as a method of thinking directed at undermining concepts that represent any feature of social reality as solid, fixed, substantial, enduring and so on. This is what gives postmodern theory its particular flavour. The sources of this methodological principle are the power attributed to signs, images, the symbolic, and a related commitment to anti-materialism, especially historical materialism, that is, Marxism. In applying this principle postmodern theory communicates an image of the world that is *liberated* from the fixities and necessities of the past. Whether or not this liberation translates into a meaningful freedom for the individual is, for postmodernists, ambiguous. For Cultural Studies, however, the freedom of the individual is a meaningful freedom.

Significantly, in its attack on concepts representing fixed entities and material structures, postmodern theory dispenses with concepts that remain highly relevant in theorising consumption. One such concept is that of need. Needs, for postmodernists, summon up images of something altogether far too *necessitating,* far too substantial and enduring, and far too suggestive of restrictions on the individual. For Baudrillard, for example, needs do not exist. Rather there is a mythology or an ideology of needs.[20] Significantly, too, the concept of need plays no part in the latest ideology of consumerism. In this and in other ways, for example the absence of any hint that consumer goods are actually produced for reasons of profit, postmodern methodology can be seen to have had a strong influence in the development of the ideology of consumerism.

Finally, postmodern theory has been credited with liberating social and cultural theory from 'the tyranny of grand narratives'. Jean-François Lyotard is widely cited as the theorist most responsible for undermining the authority of two of the most influential grand narratives – Marxism and science.[21] Lyotard himself admits that sources of the de-legitimation of science were present in the late nineteenth century. In many respects Lyotard is saying nothing new. His critique of the 'emancipatory' grand narrative is quite unoriginal. However Lyotard did reduce all theories and sciences to co-existing 'language games', each with its own rules. In more conventional language, Lyotard was merely arguing what in fact had long been taken for granted in social theory, namely that science and theory are both value-laden. But whereas this fact had not prevented theorists from trying to gain authority, amongst a public, for their theorising on the basis of strengthening their arguments, now it seems that such an approach is rendered futile by the 'fact' that language games are local and do not share the same rules. No meta-narrative or grand narrative 'could embrace the totality of metaprescriptions regulating the totality of statements circulating in the social collectivity'.[22]

Whatever encouragement the sociology of culture and Cultural Studies received from Lyotard, it is clear that an epistemological and cultural relativism has become the order of the day. There are no authoritative bases for judging the merits of truth claims or cultural values enshrined in theories. Yet people do make judgements. Now with no authority capable of legislating in these matters, the individual is, in practice, invested with the authority to decide for himself or herself. 'Truth is what I claim it to be', and what is more 'My opinions, my arguments and my theories are as valid as any others.'

The attack on grand narratives is not restricted to science and overarching theories; more importantly it is an attack on intellectual conventions that could at least distinguish opinion from theory, an incoherent argument from a coherent argument, theory from fiction, theory from reality, an intent at truthful representation from playful fiction and so on. This is the legacy of postmodern methodology. As these conventions have fallen from grace, anything goes. The green light has been given to poor scholarship, truncated thinking and weak theory. Indeed it no longer seems important to make such identifications since they presuppose the validity of the conventions that belong to an earlier era and are deemed to be no longer relevant.

In the British context, where the ideology of consumerism is most at home, institutional pressures have massively reinforced the doctrine of 'anything goes' with all its pitfalls.[23] Theories become influential, not on the basis of their intellectual merits, but on the sheer volume of the public visibility achieved as a consequence of flooding the academic market with their own local narratives. Beyond a certain volume, publicity becomes self-generating. Hence the influence of postmodern theory in Cultural Studies, and now the latest ideology of consumerism.

2 The Symbolic Value of Consumption

Current theoretical orthodoxy describes consumption as primarily, and above all else, a symbolic activity. This is typically taken to mean that when we consume we are essentially consuming symbolic meanings. Obviously we consume, amongst other things, material objects with a use value. But, for the ideology of consumerism, it is the symbolic meanings of these material objects that take pride of place in the description and explanation of consumption. The symbolic value of contemporary consumption practices, it is maintained, holds the key to explaining why people consume. This is a radical departure from common sense understandings of why we consume.

Within the ideology of consumerism, the exchange value and *material* use value of consumer products are ignored or relegated to a secondary or minor role in explaining consumption, or are themselves treated as values that cannot escape symbolisation. Consumption today is thus viewed as being grounded in the symbolic. As we shall see in following chapters, it is the alleged symbolic value of consumption that provides the latest ideology of consumerism with a framework for its theorisation of both identity construction and individual freedom. Our main concern in this chapter, however, is with the ways in which the ideology of consumerism regards the pleasures and meanings of consumption as being based on, and reflecting the symbolic nature of consumption.

Meaning and Pleasure

It will become clear shortly that current theoretical fashion overstates both the symbolic nature and symbolic value of consumption. First, however, it is necessary to identify just what the symbolic nature and value of consumption means for the ideology of consumerism.

It must be said that while there is much talk of the symbolic value of consumption there is very little that gives us a clear indication of what this actually means. Earlier attempts to give the symbolic some substantive content, as in the speculations of Roland Barthes,[1] have been more or less ditched by the latest ideology of consumerism. Thus instead of declaring that by eating steak, for example, we are actually consuming virility (its alleged symbolic value), the latest ideology of consumerism prefers a more open-ended approach to what things mean. Indeed, what things mean is no longer a concern. Rather, the ideology of consumerism emphasises meaning construction as a *process* involving the individual interacting with symbolic meanings.

Nevertheless, perhaps because of the association between the symbolic and the immaterial, unreal, hyperreal, surreal and so on, theorising consumption as a symbolic process has led, as we shall see, to some bizarre speculations. While some of the wildest theoretical excesses have become a part of the latest ideology of consumerism, whether or not they attract widespread agreement is debatable. My main concern in this chapter is with that part of the ideology which appears to be widely supported within Cultural Studies and the sociology of culture. Nevertheless it will be useful to highlight some of the more extravagant and celebratory claims of the ideology of consumerism in order better to define its consensual core.

Consumption as symbolic refers to the notion that consumption is essentially the consumption of symbolic meanings. However, as I made clear in the previous chapter, this is not understood as a passive process but rather as an active one in which the consumer is involved in a creative (and pleasurable) process of meaning negotiation and construction. Consumption is thus seen as *meaningful* and pleasurable, and it is our engagement with the symbolic that makes it so.

Viewing consumption as primarily symbolic trades on the recognition that the *images* (meanings) originally produced through advertising, and circulated through the mass media and the display of goods in shopping malls and high streets, are not only proliferating, but may (and often do) become detached from their objects – there are more signs or images in circulation than there are objects. This detachment is normally understood to be a consequence of the creative symbolic work of consumers themselves. In other words, goods and services are invested with meaning (their commodified symbolic value) by producers and advertisers. Consumers may thus consume goods for this symbolic value, or, may adopt alternative meanings that circulate throughout particular subcultures or social groupings, or may attribute their own meanings to products.

From here, the consensual position within the latest ideology of consumerism emphasises the way in which meanings and pleasures derived from consumption are used to create particular lifestyles supportive of distinctive identities. This will be the focus of the next chapter. Increasingly theorists are happy not to specify the particular meanings and pleasures that can be derived from consumption. Meanings and pleasures are, after all, a matter that can be determined only by the individual. Nevertheless, meanings and pleasures are assumed to be of central significance for individuals in their interpretation of experiences, in their making sense of the social worlds they inhabit, in organising their actions and in constituting their sense of self (self-identity).

This much is agreed. Beyond this point, however, the consensual position becomes either harder to pin down, or disappears altogether into two theoretical directions. On the one hand there are those who tend to give priority to the cognitive-moral-rational dimensions of symbolic meaning. On the other hand there are academics who privilege the aesthetic-emotional-irrational dimensions of pleasure. In the former, the symbolic value of consumption is explored in ways that both assume and lend support to the idea that the individual is essentially a rational, decision-making being. In the latter, the bodily and cerebral pleasures of consumption are closely tied in to the manner in which the intense imagery of consumer culture summons up dreams, fantasies and desires.

On the face of it, it would seem that the consensus that forms the core of the ideology of consumerism breaks up into two emphases reflecting two distinct approaches to human motivations – one based on meaning and making sense, the other on pleasure and desire. Of course there is no necessary incompatibility here. Clearly pleasures can be derived from the act of creating meaning and meaning can be achieved in the pursuit of pleasure. More than this, the complexity of human motivations does allow scope for the rational and irrational to co-exist within the individual.

The theoretical consensus does not seem to have a problem with this. Indeed, it is increasingly the case that the ideology of consumerism subsumes all sources of motivation to those directly relevant to self-identity. Thus rather than opting for a view that locates the attractions of consumption in either meaning or pleasure, the tendency is to acknowledge that their relevance will vary in relation to the preferences of individuals. Such a move allows the consensus not to specify the substantive content of the symbolic, leaving the latter to the individual consumer. The consensus is unwilling to embrace those theoretical speculations that might be perceived to lack credibility and hence attract criticism. The consumer, however, given the commitment of Cultural Studies to anti-elitism, is assumed to be beyond criticism.

The cognitive-moral-rational direction to theorising the symbolic value of consumption has its roots in earlier Cultural Studies work on youth subcultures, such as mods and rockers.[2] In that era Cultural Studies acknowledged the existence of a dominant culture with its attendant dominant ideology (values and *meanings*). Certain youth subcultures were seen as consciously developing a style that purposefully subverted, or even contradicted, dominant meanings. Given the political significance that Cultural Studies attributes to ideology (its ideology-centredness), it is unsurprising that stylistic consumption that contested commodified meanings should be seen as 'political'. With hindsight, however, we can say that mods and rockers may have had some cultural significance, but to depict this as politically significant is to stretch the bounds of credibility.

In more recent times there are still those who treat forms of stylistic consumption that contest commodified symbolic values as political. Arguably the most bizarre expression of this view is to be found in the writings of John Fiske who sees shopping as *the* site of political conflict and struggle. Shopping 'is where the art and tricks of the weak can inflict most damage on, and exert most power over, the strategic interests of the powerful'.[3] He refers to young people as 'shopping mall guerrillas par excellence',[4] and women, that is 'the weak', are accorded a similar status. While the theoretical consensus around consumption does explicitly distance itself from Fiske's extravagant assertions, it does come perilously close, as we shall see in the next chapter, to adopting an identical stance in theorising the role that consumption plays in the so-called politics of identity.

With regard to the aesthetic-emotional-irrational dimensions of pleasure, the consensus acknowledges the postmodern emphasis on the aestheticisation of everyday life. It thus goes along with Mike Featherstone's view that 'The centrality of the commercial manipulation of images through advertising, the media and the displays, performances and spectacles of the urbanized fabric of daily life ... entails a constant re-working of desires through images.' The consensus, too, seems to agree that 'the consumer society ...

confronts people with dream-images which speak to desires, and aestheticize and de-realize reality'.[5]

However, the consensus appears to part company with Featherstone and others in its attempts to link the aestheticisation of everyday life to actual consumption practices. 'The aestheticization of everyday life,' Featherstone tells us, 'can refer to the project of turning life into a work of art'. One example of such a project was that of dandyism, which amongst other things, manifested 'the heroic concern with the achievement of originality and superiority in dress, demeanour, personal habits and even furnishings – what we now call lifestyle'.[6]

Featherstone provides historical examples of 'artistic and intellectual counter-cultures', which pursued a 'dual focus on a life of aesthetic consumption and the need to form life into an aesthetically pleasing whole'. But this dual focus, Featherstone suggests, 'should be related to the development of mass consumption in general and the pursuit of new tastes and sensations and the construction of distinctive lifestyles which has become central to consumer culture'.[7] The consensus is happy enough to go along with this provided that it remains as a comment that is specific to particular groups. Consumer-based lifestyles as works of art may be descriptive of the lifestyles pursued by very small groups. When this observation is *generalised* and aligned with the notion of 'the artist as hero' in the context of the growing aestheticisation of everyday life and consumer-based lifestyles, Featherstone is but a short step away from celebrating contemporary consumption as heroic and the consumer as a hero![8] While the consensus does celebrate consumption, to follow Featherstone all the way would be a case of the celebration 'going over the top'.

The theoretical consensus which forms the core of the latest ideology of consumerism appears to prefer an understanding of the symbolic value of consumption that retains an openness and flexibility sufficient seemingly to accommodate whatever meanings and pleasures the individual consumer can derive or create from consuming. But, as we shall see shortly, this is far from the case. The very assumption that consumption is *primarily* a symbolic activity does propel theory in a direction that discounts those meanings and pleasures, for example, practically-based meanings and uncomplicated fun, which may well be of considerable relevance to consumers. In doing this the ideology of consumerism makes itself vulnerable to serious criticisms. In exploring some of these criticisms

I will raise the following questions. To what extent is consumption symbolic? Has everyday life been increasingly aestheticised by consumer culture? Are the pleasures of consumption aesthetically-based? How meaningful are the meanings and pleasures derived from consumption?

Consumption as Symbolic?

There is no need to deny that everything that is produced and consumed carries meanings. There is no need, either, to deny the fact that these meanings are culturally-based and arbitrary, that is they can vary according to the values of particular cultures. We can, along with Marshall Sahlins, say that it is cultural values and meanings that provide the reasons why 'Americans deem dogs inedible and cattle "food"',[9] or why, in most if not all cultures, trousers are deemed to be masculine and skirts feminine. Obviously cultural values and meanings play a significant role in both the production and consumption of goods. The important question is: how significant?

For the ideology of consumerism, cultural values and meanings are prioritised in both the description and explanation of consumption and production. Sahlins asserts that:

> Production is a functional moment of a cultural structure. This understood, the rationality of the market and of bourgeois society is put in another light. The famous logic of maximisation is only the manifest reason of another Reason ... It is not as if we had no culture: no symbolic code of objects – in relation to which the mechanism of supply-demand-price, ostensibly in command, is in reality the servant.[10]

Now, contemporary ideologues, it must be said, do not attempt to ground their assumption of the primacy of the symbolic value of goods as Sahlins does – they merely assume this primacy as a self-evident truth. It is nevertheless useful to examine this alleged self-evident truth in the light of the kind of thinking advanced by Sahlins – not that Sahlins is particularly influential, but his thinking is symptomatic of the kind of thinking that has produced the latest ideology of consumerism.

In making his case for symbolic values shaping the exchange value and use value of what is produced and consumed, Sahlins offers an analysis of the production and consumption of meat. This is a well-chosen example. Food, after all, is universally considered to be necessary (absolutely useful) for our survival. The general use value of food is beyond question, as too is clothing for protection from the elements. If Sahlins can 'prove' that cultural codes govern the utility of products that are uncontroversially perceived to be consumed in order to meet a basic need, then he will have totally undermined commonsensical explanations of consumption.

Sahlins, in constructing his proof, quite correctly observes that the popularity of certain meats bears no relation to their nutritional (use) value.

> It is the symbolic logic which organises demand. The social value of steak or roast, as compared with tripe or tongue, is what underlies the difference in economic value. From the nutritional point of view, such a notion of 'better' and 'inferior' cuts would be difficult to defend. Moreover, steak remains the most expensive meat even though its absolute supply is much greater than that of tongue ...[11]

The consumption of meat, at least in the American context, would seem to obey the logic of cultural values rather than the logic of needs. Or, in other words, the use value of meat is shaped by symbolic values. Now, while we can think of examples in which actual purchases reflect symbolic values *only* (the replica football shirt), and examples in which symbolic values outweigh considerations of utiliy (the purchase of an expensive, luxury sports car), it would be a mistake to assume that such examples are typical of *all* consumption. On closer inspection these examples are the exception rather than the rule.

Sahlins has 'demonstrated' that use values in the consumption of meat are culturally coded – and that is all that he has demonstrated. But Sahlins uses the example of meat as *typical* of the consumption of food in general, and *all consumption*. This is unjustified. Then, having mistakenly arrived at a theory of consumption Sahlins goes on to draw on uncontroversial examples, such as trousers and skirts, to support his theory. The initial error of generalising from the example of meat can be recognised if we ask: what are the cultural codes governing the consumption of vegetables, fruit, cereals, sandwiches, etc? While cultural codes appear to have relevance in the consumption of clothes, for example, one would be hard pressed to identify equivalent codes relevant to refrigerators, freezers, cookers, fuel, or most other things for that matter. Even with over-imaged commodities, such as cars, it is impossible, without being incredulously speculative, to identify the symbolic code that accounts for *all* of the differences between cars.

Advocates of the latest ideology of consumerism could claim that they have moved on from Sahlins and therefore my criticisms of Sahlins are not relevant to the current orthodoxy. As I noted earlier the symbolic is no longer restricted to 'objective' cultural *codes* – the symbolic today is understood more as an open-ended interpretative process. This means that the ideology of consumerism avoids the error of assuming that the motive to consume can be read off the particular cultural codes attributed to particular commodities.

However, it fails to recognise the error of generalising from specific examples, as in generalising from the highly stylised consumption of youth subcultures. It assumes that all consumption is governed by symbolic processes. It also replicates the error of using atypical instances of stylised consumption to support its false assumption that all consumption is stylised. More than this, it radicalises Sahlins' claim that use values are ordered by cultural values. First, by more or less getting rid of the social content of cultural values in favour of a symbolic process in which the social itself becomes one of a multitude of images; and second, by obliterating the concept of use value from its account of consumption. If the utility of a commodity is governed by symbolic values, then, for the ideology of con-sumerism, there is no point in even considering the mundane world of use values. Clearly whatever the symbolic differences between goods, whether cuts of meat, clothes or cars, almost all goods retain a use value.

As we shall see later, material use values (irrespective of the extent to which the use values themselves, or the products consumed are drenched in symbolic values), are, for most purchases and for most consumers, prioritised. Indeed, it is typically, though not always, the material use value of a commodity that renders its consumption *meaningful*. In ignoring use values, the ideology of consumerism is ignoring the most important and the most credible ways in which consumption can be said to be meaningful. Instead, especially in the pleasures of consumption approach, meaning is reduced to the symbolic, to images and to free-floating signs. These signs may well be understood as trans-coded, which, of course, multiplies their meaning. But these meanings, while perhaps no longer understood as semiotically-generated, are nevertheless understood in the same restrictive sense.

What these comments allude to is two quite distinct concepts of meaning – the restricted semiotic, text-based concept, and the social, practical concept. These correspond to two different concepts of culture – the former as de-materialised, even abstract, images and symbols; the latter as a way of life. When the ideology of consumerism claims to have based itself on the everyday practices of ordinary people,[12] it is at its most confusing. It is concerned only with those practices that can be understood via the restricted concept of meaning.

Needless to say, a semiotically derived concept of meaning is essentially irrelevant to the concept of meaning that is based in practical, social lives. I might claim, for example, that buying a new car *means* that I can now be more assured that I can reliably get from A to B than was the case with my old car. A semiotically derived concept of meaning can make no sense of this. It may, however, read something into the colour and shape of the car, perhaps linking this with virility, aggression, sexual motivation and so on. These images or symbols are supposedly the resources out of which meaning is made. Seeing the consumer as a meaning-maker is not a problem. But understanding this process as involving a playful interaction with commodified symbolic values most certainly is when the latter are irrelevant to the consumer.

As we saw in the previous chapter, the latest ideology of consumerism tends toward the view that the meaning of things is infinite, that is, things or objects are open to an infinite range of meanings. But, as I have argued, this ideology does exclude from consideration those meanings that derive from the practical use value of the product. The symbolic nature of consumption, for the ideology of consumerism, does *not* refer to the whole range of potential meanings and pleasures that can be derived from consuming, but rather to *specific meanings and pleasures* which may or may not be relevant to the consumer.

The Aestheticisation of Everyday Life ?

The pleasure of consumption strand of the ideology of consumerism does embody a range of theoretical emphases. Michel de Certeau and his followers, for example, focus on consumption as a meaningful process involving creative tactics and strategies.[13] In the hands of

John Fiske, as I noted earlier, these tactics and strategies are attributed with a political relevance. A somewhat different, but nevertheless compatible, view is that advanced by Colin Campbell. He sees consumption as an expression of hedonistic desires, and theorises in some detail how modern forms of hedonism are influenced by consumer culture.[14] And there are those, like George Ritzer, who focus on consumption as fun and entertainment. 'Consumption has less and less to do with obtaining goods and services and more to do with entertainment.'[15]

Ritzer's work, however, is of limited value for the *whole* of the ideology of consumerism. Quite simply he tends to view the consumer as *manipulated* by the lure of displayed goods.

> The cathedrals of consumption can be seen as great stage sets that are constructed to lure consumers and extract their money. Employees are increasingly actors who may well be in costume and speak scripted lines. Consumers are made to feel part of the show, at least for the time they are in the cathedral.[16]

As we shall see, the ideology of consumerism, in its attempt to explain consumption in terms of the pleasures anticipated and experienced, has to steer an awkward path. Quite simply the sources of pleasures made available by consumer culture must be understood in ways that render them to be non-trivial. If the pleasures to be had from consuming are theorised as trivial, the explanation of consumption based on anticipated and experienced trivial pleasures loses its power and credibility. Besides, it would imply that consumers are trivial, and this cannot be countenanced. Arguably the most popular attempt to overcome this problem is to treat the sources of pleasure as arising from an increasingly aestheticised consumer culture and the consequent aestheticisation of everyday life.

The aestheticisation of everyday life, as noted earlier, can refer to treating one's life as a work of art. The range of goods available today, it is argued, enable more people to engage in such a pleasurable project. As a 'work of art' the pleasures derived from creating a consumer-based lifestyle are supposedly meaningful rather than trivial. The aestheticisation of everyday life thesis, however, does include two other kinds of argument. A second sense in which everyday life can be said to be aestheticised, according to Featherstone, arises from that activity associated with artistic subcultures which 'sought in their work, writings, and in some cases lives, to efface the boundary between art and everyday life'. Influential here is the challenge to traditional definitions of art itself, such that 'art can be anywhere or anything'.[17] This means that consumer objects can be treated as art.

The third sense in which it is argued that everyday life is aestheticised focuses on 'the rapid flow of signs and images which saturate the fabric of everyday life'.[18] These images are those transmitted by advertising (in its broadest sense), and in some cases are influenced by the techniques of artistic subcultures.

The aestheticisation of everyday life thesis generates an understanding of the pleasurable and meaningful nature of consumption as somehow rooted in our interaction with aesthetics. On the face of it this thesis would seem to have some merit and it does complement trends in Cultural Studies. The thesis does attempt to support the notion that the aesthetic pleasures facilitated by consumer culture are meaningful. Important here is the 'widely recognised', at least in postmodern theory, collapse of the boundary between serious art and popular art. Many advertisements, particularly televised advertisements, are regarded as influential in the merging of serious and popular art forms. On top of this, there has been, at least in Cultural Studies and some other quarters, a broadening of the definition of what can legitimately be called art – popular or 'light' cultural products are amenable to the same kind of serious attention once reserved for serious art. The consequent 'merging' of the serious and the popular in what is regarded as the aesthetic realm infuses everyday reality as never before in the escalation of advertising and in the sites of consumption. Almost all shops attempt to appeal to consumers through window displays that are 'aesthetically inviting', through the display of goods that are pleasing to the eye and through the playing of music.

Ironically, the aestheticisation of everyday life thesis does retain an important, powerful role for advertising. But this power is not construed in terms of manipulating the consumer, but more in terms of offering enticing images that, in effect, are the aesthetic resources which we are able to use to inspire or re-route our dreams, fantasies and desires. It can be noted that there is a strong tendency amongst advocates of the thesis to prefer to talk of dreams, fantasies and desires rather than simple enjoyment and fun. The former have a serious, and thus more meaningful, conceptual history, especially in their association with 'serious' psychoanalytic theory. And, of course, they are associated with *powerful* psychological motives. Our powerful motives thus interact with the powerful images of consumer culture. For Featherstone the latter are so powerful that

> ... it is important to stress that ... it needs discipline and control to stroll through goods on display, to look and not snatch, to move casually without interrupting the flow, to gaze with controlled enthusiasm and a blasé outlook, to observe others without being seen, to tolerate the close proximity of bodies without feeling threatened. It also requires the capacity to manage swings between intense involvement and more distanced aesthetic detachment.[19]

Additionally, certain consumer products themselves contribute to the so-called growing aestheticisation of everyday life. Televisions, radios, personal stereos and music centres are obvious examples. They enable access to cultural products, some of which are aesthetically overloaded, as in radio and television programmes that are unnecessarily shot through with music. And if a pile of bricks or dog shit can be transformed into a work of art, or even seen as such, so too can a house. Each of its rooms can be aetheticised. The availability of DIY tools and materials enables this. Numerous other examples of the aestheticisation of everyday life, from quadrophonic sounds spilling out of cars to the particular decor and music of theme pubs, from the wide range of styles and colours in cars and clothes to the colourful presentation of exotic foods, can be cited to compile an impressive dossier of evidence in support of the aestheticisation of everyday life thesis.

Given the pervasiveness of aesthetic values, and their close association with meaningful pleasures, it is difficult to imagine how consumption could be anything but pleasurable in ways that are sufficiently meaningful to ensure that the motive to consume is unproblematically rooted in the aesthetic value of consumption. It would thus seem that in its emphasis on the meaningful pleasures of consumption the ideology of consumerism is not an ideology after all, but a theory offering a credible explanation of consumption. However, such an estimation cannot be further from the truth. The aestheticisation of everyday life thesis is a convenient myth that falsely upgrades the pleasures of consumption.

I appreciate that any dismissal of the validity of the aestheticisation of everyday life thesis is more or less guaranteed to attract the charge of elitism. Apart from a few diehard cultural conservatives, of both left-wing and right-wing persuasions, nobody dares to challenge this thesis. To make this challenge invariably involves the raising of distinctions, and the values underpinning them, that are widely regarded as being untenable. I am thinking here of the distinctions that were once (but now no longer) routinely made between 'true' or serious art on the one hand, and popular or light art on the other. Unfortunately, this distinction was almost universally (mis)understood as reflecting the value-laden distinction between highbrow and lowbrow culture and their close identification with the bourgeoisie and the masses. The anti-elitism of Cultural Studies quite rightly railed against this. But, as I argued in the previous chapter, Cultural Studies has gradually adopted an uncritical populism that rules out the legitimacy of making qualitative judgements about popular cultural products. The aestheticisation of everyday life thesis falls into the same trap and provides a spurious grounding for the ideology of consumerism.

The aestheticisation of everyday life thesis refuses to make judgements either about the aesthetic status of the images of consumer culture or about the pleasures to be had from interacting with these images. But it nevertheless *assumes* that meaningful pleasures are facilitated by the aesthetic imagery of consumer culture. This assumption, which has little empirical support, is based on a series of loose associations that implicitly trade on the recognised aesthetic value of art – life as art, the techniques of artistic subcultures, artistic imagery, art as meaningful – while explicitly denying this value. This denial allows the aesthetic value of consumer culture to be of equal status to that of art. In other words the aesthetic status of the imagery of consumer culture is elevated. This is unwarranted.

First, aesthetic resources do vary in terms of their capacity to enable pleasures. It is widely recognised that cultural products such as films, plays, novels and so on vary in their capacity to promote self-engagement, absorption, contemplation and reflection. While individuals do react and interact differently in relation to specific cultural products, the meaning of the pleasures derived is invariably related to the individual's level of self-engagement and absorption. It thus seems somewhat odd that the meaningful pleasures of consumption are so closely tied in to particular aesthetic resources, that is signs and images, that have a restricted capacity for promoting meaningful pleasures. The display and packaging of goods cannot be aesthetically equated with those cultural products that do promote an enduring involvement. In spite of 'textualisation', signs and images *are* signs and images. No amount of theorising about the 'artistic' techniques involved in the production of images can alter this fact.

The kind of judgement involved in determining the relative value of commodities or experiences for meaningful pleasures, aesthetic or otherwise, is in fact one that is commonly made. The football purist, for example, will eulogise about the 'poetry' or other aesthetic delights provided by the Dutch national team of 1974, the Brazilians of 1982, Liverpool of 1989 and Real Madrid of 2000, and bemoan the standardised dross of much professional football. For the spectator (consumer) of this standardised product aesthetic pleasures are few and far between, perhaps a few isolated moments of eye-catching and pleasing skill.

Second, the example of football illustrates the obvious fact that aesthetically irrelevant pleasures may be far more common than the anticipated and experienced pleasures of an aesthetic variety. For the typical football fan, with aesthetic pleasures more or less ruled out, and unanticipated, the pleasures of attending a match are more likely to derive from the experience of the atmosphere generated by the crowd, from chanting and cheering or having a moan, from verbally abusing the referee, players, or opposing fans, and most of all from the team's victory. The aestheticisation of everyday life thesis says nothing about these kinds of pleasures. It says nothing about most of the little pleasures that are widely experienced through consumption – the pleasures initially experienced, for example, in replacing old, inefficient products with more reliable and efficient ones, or from 'getting a bargain', or from purchasing a gift for a loved one, or from just having fun with the kids at a theme park and so on. Presumably, for the ideology of consumerism, these kinds of pleasures don't have the same kind of status and power as grand-sounding aesthetic pleasures.

It ought to be clear that I am not denying that pleasures can be experienced from consumption. I am, however, questioning the ideology of consumerism's tendency to theorise the pleasures of consumption as essentially aesthetically-based. This may hold true for specific forms of consumption for a small minority of consumers. And, when this is true, it is most unlikely to take a form that corresponds to the aestheticisation of everyday life thesis. This brings me to my third point. The aestheticisation of everyday life thesis is not particularly sensitive to the fact that the packaging and presentation of commodities, the glitz of shopping malls and advertisements, televisual and otherwise, constitute, for some at least, not so much evidence of aestheticisation but rather visual pollution. Similarly one person's (or one shop's) music is another person's irritating noise.

Fourth, in equating the aesthetic with the imagery of consumer culture, the aestheticisation of everyday life thesis is in fact re-defining the aesthetic in terms of the decorative and superficial, that is, in terms that denude the aesthetic of the content that renders it meaningful. Indeed, Featherstone refers to 'the playful exploration of transitory experiences and surface aesthetic effects' involved in 'the active stylization of life'.[20] Yet, the ideology of consumerism insists on the importance of this for consumers. Incoherently it is insisting on a nonsense – the significance of the insignificant, the importance of the trivial.

Finally, if 'anything can be art' and 'art is everywhere', why does the aestheticisation of everyday life thesis focus on consumer culture? The aesthetically meaningful would seem far more likely to be experienced in ways that have very little to do with consumption.

Meanings, Pleasures and the Meaningful

My arguments throughout this chapter suggest that consumption can be experienced as both meaningful and pleasurable, but *not* in ways proposed by the ideology of consumerism. We have seen that the latter embraces an understanding of the value of consumer culture for facilitating pleasures that is unconvincing. Likewise it theorises the meaningful nature of consumption in highly specific ways that seem to have little relevance for most consumers. We can make some sense of this in the context of the evolution of Cultural Studies and the sociology of culture, outlined in the previous chapter. However, we can go further than this in attempting to identify why it is that the ideology of consumerism insists on depicting consumption as meaningful and pleasurable in ways that do not ring true. In what follows I shall argue that the ideology of consumerism adopts a concept of 'the meaningful' that is essentially divorced from *experience*, and it is this that enables it to present a distorted picture of the meaningful nature of consumption.

As I noted earlier the ideology of consumerism operates with two distinct concepts of meaning. It not only tends to slide between the two concepts in ways that are inappropriate, it also fails to realise that the concept of 'the meaningful' cannot be derived from either of the two concepts of meaning. It is just this – the assumption that 'the meaningful' is an automatic product of the process of making sense or meaning – that can be identified as the main source of the ideology of consumerism's peculiar approach to consumption as meaningful.

On the face of it, it might seem perfectly reasonable to assume that the meaningful is a product of meaning construction. If consumption involves a meaning-maker (the consumer) interacting with commodities that are full of meaning, is this not the same as saying that consumption is meaning*ful?* We can answer this in the affirmative only if we are prepared to use a concept of the meaningful that not only radically departs from normal usage, but does so in ways that lose the significance of the latter. The process of meaning construction is, in fact, unremarkable. It is something we all do, more or less continuously and routinely, and more often than not, tacitly. If we want to refer to the product of this process as 'meaningful' then we have to acknowledge that 'the meaningful' is likewise unremarkable. Whether or not our meaning construction processes actually generate 'the meaningful', in the more typical use of the term, is an open question. Since the process of meaning construction is more or less continuous, and since a small proportion only of our experiences tend to merit the judgement of meaningful, it is clear that 'the meaningful' as experienced is not the same as the product of meaning construction. In other words when the ideology of consumerism claims that consumption is a meaningful activity it is using a concept of 'the meaningful' that is substantially irrelevant to what 'the meaningful' is normally taken to mean. This is a clear case of a major misleading claim of the ideology of consumerism.

In its normal usage 'the meaningful' is differentiated from the mundane and the unremarkable. Indeed, the latter are more typically associated with meaninglessness. When we refer to a meaningful experience we do so following an assessment of the quality of the experience that differentiates it from the mundane and unremarkable. In other words, to declare an experience to be meaningful (or to have been meaningful) is to make a judgement about the quality of the experience in question. This judgement is a thoroughly subjective one and can be made only by the individual. All sorts of considerations influence this judgement, but it inherently involves comparison with other experiences, in the context of the individual's totality of experiences, and in relation to the individual's own sense of priorities.

The ideology of consumerism's failure to appreciate all that is involved in making judgements about the relative meaningfulness or otherwise of our experiences is partially disguised by claims that it is, in fact, a theory that is based on empirical evidence of the consumption practices of 'ordinary people' in their everyday lives. In other words, advocates of the ideology of consumerism claim that a number of studies reveal that 'the meaningful' as a product of meaning construction is actually 'the meaningful' as experienced.[21] This claim, I will argue, is invalid.

These studies, normally referred to as 'ethnographic', are more sensitive to the experience of those being studied than the traditional empirical methods of surveys and formal questionnaires. Ethnographic studies ideally involve researchers in informal communicative interaction with those being studied. Typically however, the purpose of the ethnographic study is *not* to 'discover' the research subjects' own ways of representing their experiences and actions, *but only those ways that are relevant to the 'topic' of the study.* It is thus already potentially distanced from the individual research subject's own priorities. This sets up the possibility that the ethnographic study is researching representations of experiences that are actually experienced as irrelevant and meaningless.

While social scientists accept that ethnographic studies do not produce generalisable results, we have already noted that this limitation has not prevented Cultural Studies academics from generalising from examples of highly specific forms of consumption to all consumption and all consumers. As we know from the critique of more traditional research methodologies, the interests of the researcher, let alone his or her own values, do distort research outcomes. The potential for undisclosed distortion in the 'looser' ethnographic study is far greater than in more formal studies. Quite clearly when in researching consumption practices, if the meaningful, or meaningful pleasures, do not reflect the subjective assessments of research subjects, but are nevertheless reported as such, the findings merely reflect and support the researcher's own inadequate conception of 'the meaningful'.

The claim that ethnographic studies support the ideology of consumerism's emphasis on the symbolic nature and symbolic value of consumption is thus not only highly misleading, it is also mystifying. To avoid this mystification ethnographic research should attempt to uncover the meaningful and the pleasurable as experienced, regardless of their sources. As we shall see later this suggests that 'life-satisfaction' studies offer a more valid means of assessing the role of consumption, and the nature of its pleasures and meaningfulness. Without pre-empting later discussion, it can be noted here that the evidence of these studies offers very little support for the ideology of consumerism.

In an academic environment in which 'anything goes' bad theory can readily isolate itself from criticism – all the more so if the bad theory becomes fashionable. This is unsurprising. Within all academic fields there is a long history of the once popular and fashionable being replaced by a new perspective. Where relevant the new perspective, or paradigm, bases its ascendancy on being better able, perhaps by being more comprehensive and coherent, to explain existing evidence. What is disturbing about the ideology of consumerism is that it is a theory that is underinformed by *appropriate* empirical evidence. It thus immunises itself against both theoretical criticism and the 'reality-check' of relevant empirical evidence. As we shall see in the next chapter, instead of submitting itself to the test of appropriate empirical evidence, the ideology of consumerism reinforces its own misconceptions about the meaningful nature of consumption in its theorisation of the value of consumption for self-identity.

3 Consumption, Identity and Lifestyle

The latest ideology of consumerism does not rest its claims that consumption is meaningful solely on the kinds of arguments considered in the previous chapter. Far more common today is the view that what makes consumption meaningful is that it speaks directly to the self. Our most important meanings are widely regarded as those that constitute our selves. The ideology of consumerism has it that it is primarily through consumption that we become who we are and display who we are.

In the words of Hugh Mackay, who is somewhat crudely paraphrasing the work of Pierre Bourdieu, 'Consumption is the articulation of a sense of identity. Our identity is made up by our consumption of goods – and their consumption and display constitutes our expression of taste.'[1] Daniel Miller, in the same textbook, tells students that one of the main aims of his chapter is 'to change how you think about consumption from being merely the act of buying goods to being a fundamental process by which we create identity'.[2] In another introductory textbook, Robert Bocock, who is critical of consumerism, concludes that 'It is because consumption has entered the processes of identity formation and identity maintenance, that it has become so central to people's lives in western capitalism.'[3]

The view that consumption is the principal means through which we construct, maintain, reconstruct and display our identities has become the most important element of the latest ideology of consumerism. Consumer motivations are to be understood not only in terms of the symbolic meanings and pleasures made available by consumption, but ultimately in terms of the central relevance of consumption for our identities. As such, the ideology of consumerism offers what it sees as a very powerful explanation of consumption. Yet, at the very same time, this 'explanation' serves to promote consumerism.

Quite simply, issues concerning self-identity have, in recent times, become socially significant. There is a growing academic literature within social and cultural theory that attempts to analyse why this is so. For the moment, however, we can note that there is general agreement that our strongest motivations are wrapped up in our self-identities. Clearly, in stressing the identity value of consumption, the ideology of consumerism is aligning itself with what is becoming increasingly important in people's lives.

I do not dispute the increasing social prominence of issues relevant to self-identity. But I do take issue with the assumed close connection between identity construction and consumerism. Indeed I shall argue that this alleged close connection is the exception rather than the rule. My main criticism of the ideology of consumerism's pronouncements on the positive value of consumption for identity is that sources of self-identity other than consumerism are ignored. The alleged basis of self-identity in consumer culture does marginalise all other, and far more important, sources of identity. This steers the ideology of consumerism toward adopting a concept of identity that is essentially superficial and trivial, one that effectively transforms the concept of identity into image, while drawing on the social and personal significance of the former.

The ideology of consumerism, in its emphasis on 'stylised' consumption, does make a limited attempt to protect itself from such criticism. But I shall argue that the work on stylised consumption actually reinforces my criticisms. More than this, this work constitutes a celebration of self-alienation. However, it is the *only* body of work supportive of the ideology of consumerism's treatment of identity that draws on empirical studies. For the most part the ideology's claims are empirically unsupported. What we do get, as we shall see below, are unfounded assertions stating the positive identity value of consumerism.

The Social Significance of Identity

We can begin to get some idea of the distinctiveness of the latest ideology of consumerism's position on the identity value of consumption by noting its break with earlier thinking on this matter. This break revolves around two axes. First, whereas the identity value of consumption was mainly articulated in terms of the achievement of social prestige and the display of hierarchically ordered social status, the latest ideology of consumerism prefers to emphasise the value of consumption for the constitution and display of difference, understood non-judgementally, with no reference to social hierarchies. Thus Thorstein Veblen's famous study in which he specified the ways in which 'useless' consumption was used by the emerging 'leisure class' at the end of the nineteenth century to express 'superior' social status, is of historical interest only.[4]

The ideology of consumerism has a more ambiguous relationship with the work of Pierre Bourdieu, who, more than anyone else, has charted the interconnections between class cultures, consumption and identities.[5] On the one hand his analysis of 'taste' and 'style' does elevate the significance of the culture of commodities to a central place in the constitution and expression of class and personal identities. The ideology of consumerism is more than happy with the emphasis on style, but finds Bourdieu's work too restrictive in so far as his class-based analysis not only ignores the role of gender and race, but importantly here, promotes the view that taste and style are hierarchically ordered.[6] This grates with the anti-elitism informing the latest ideology of consumerism.

Noticeably, class analysis has been ditched by the ideology of consumerism. This is consistent with the second axis of the break with earlier studies. This axis revolves around a shift in emphasis from social identity to self-identity. Of course social identity, or more precisely our social identifications, are part and parcel of our self-identities. But the emphasis on self-identity not only reflects and cashes in on its growing social significance – Zygmunt Bauman critically refers to 'the individualized society'[7] – it is also intended to capture the view that the self has become a reflexive project.[8] In other words the self has increasingly become the main site on which we exercise autonomous agency. This view is consistent with the ideology of consumerism's wish to avoid any hint of socially manipulated consumption. It prefers instead to emphasise the capacity of consumer culture to cater for everybody by offering choices which allow *all individuals* to choose their self-identities and express their difference from others.

This emphasis does gain some support from recent attempts to revise self-identity theory. These revisions, it has been widely argued, do need to account for what appears to be a growing absorption with self-identity, not only among the populations of the more affluent societies, but globally. It is fair to say that issues relevant to self-identity have taken up an increasing proportion of media space and time during the past 40 years or so. While much of this attention is centred on appearance, image and style, we have also witnessed a growing coverage, not always in trivial ways, of more substantial identity matters. During the latter part of this period, too, there has been a noticeable growth in the market for self-help literature focused on identity issues and problems, from beauty tips to help with coping with anxieties that reach into the core of the self. Additionally a self-identity industry, including health clubs, fitness gyms, therapy centres, beauty salons, cosmetic surgeries and so on, has sprung up to cash in on our self-preoccupations.

All contemporary theories of identity acknowledge this growing interest in self-identity issues. How this is to be explained, however, is another matter. My purpose here is not to evaluate the explanations on offer, but to argue that there are certain emphases within current thinking about self-identity that are used by the ideology of consumerism to promote the identity value of consumption. At the same time there is much in contemporary theories of self-identity that the ideology of consumerism prefers to ignore.

Consumption as Self-liberation

The growing preoccupation with self-identity, many agree, is best understood as a consequence of those social changes, discussed in Chapter 1, which have prompted references to 'new times', late modernity or postmodernity. These changes, it is maintained, have destroyed the foundations on which identities were formed and maintained, thereby creating the need for new self-identities and new means of identity construction. But it is also argued that new opportunities have emerged which enable individuals to 'solve' this problem. However, the new opportunities arise in a rapidly changing social context and are no longer anchored in traditions. Many see this as a process in which individuals are liberated from the hold of the authority of traditions and cast into a world of uncertainties. Sure enough there are plenty of authorities (experts) around to help us pick our way through these uncertainties, but the experts are often in conflict with each other. Consequently, in the final analysis, the individual must decide for himself or herself who to be. Inevitably this generates a self-orientation focused on self-identity.

Oddly enough, for the ideology of consumerism, these new opportunities tend to be confined to those offered by consumer culture! In other words, consumer culture provides the resources that enable us to choose and express our self-identities. Consumer culture thus becomes *the* solution to 'identity-crisis'. However, consumer culture is dynamic, that is, forever changing and producing something new. Its solution to identity-crisis is thus not that of offering the self new, stable, foundations. Rather, it offers fluid and shifting foundations that enable the self continually to 're-fashion' itself in relation to a changing society.

Thus for the ideology of consumerism the positive identity value of consumption is realised in the choices we make. Choosing one's self is bound up with the choices we make in consumption. While there are many who are justifiably critical of the consequences of identity construction taking a commodified form, advocates of the ideology of consumerism are more celebratory. It is widely noted that the symbolic differences of commodities can key in rather neatly with the self's own assertion of its difference from others – an integral feature of the process of choosing one's identity. For Charlie Leadbetter this means that 'Choice in consumption, lifestyle, sexuality is more important as an assertion of identity. The dynamic area of most people's lives is where they can assert their difference from others.'[9]

Of course the construction of self-identity, and with it lifestyle choices, does not have to be closely interwoven with consumption. The existence of poverty clearly indicates that the range of identity and lifestyle choices based on consumption is severely restricted for the poor. The obviousness of this point, however, is lost in the more positive assessments of the identity value of consumption. Commenting on what he sees as a growing 'preoccupation with consumption and style', Stuart Hall notes:

> ... the fact is that greater and greater numbers of people ... play the game of using things to signify who they are. *Everybody* [my emphasis], including people in very poor societies whom we in the West frequently speak about as if they inhabit a world outside of culture, knows that today's 'goods' double up as social signs and produce meanings as well as energy.[10]

In a similar vein, consumption is, for Frank Mort,

> where people choose to put their energies and invest their hopes ... [It is] in the world of holidays, home interiors and superstores, that they have a sense of power and freedom to express themselves, to define their sense of self, to mould the good life.[11]

This kind of assertion does return us to a familiar problem.

Identity or Image?

In Chapter 1, I suggested that postmodern theories of identity, in assuming that today the sources of identity reside in the world of images, symbols and signs, postulate today's individual as a somewhat superficial being. It was also noted that such a view does pose a serious difficulty for the ideology of consumerism. It is obviously problematic to reconcile claims that the main motive to consume is based on consumerism's positive identity value when the identity in question is superficial. In the previous chapter attempts to provide the symbolic with serious substance, and thus as anything but superficial, were found wanting.

Yet, against the obvious criticism that it harbours a trivial concept of identity, the ideology of consumerism continues to insist that this is not so. This insistence, it must be said, is not rooted in a coherent theory of identity. Rather the charge of triviality is countered by drawing on the internal coherence of *stylised* consumption. Celia Lury, for example, has devoted a book to 'the way in which consumer culture' provides 'the resources for an increasingly stylized relation between an individual and his or her self-identity'. For Lury this 'stylized relation' is an important 'aspect of the refiguring of the social field'.[12]

Linking self-identity with stylised consumption, to those unfamiliar with Cultural Studies (and contemporary advertising techniques), would seem to confirm what we suspected all along: that the ideology of consumerism does indeed adopt a trivial concept of identity. To the ordinary mortal, style is all about image, and images are shallow. As we shall see later, what is meant by stylised consumption does revolve around image and style but in a way intended to make them important for the individual's non-trivial self-identity.

In order to understand better what is meant by stylised consumption, and the ideology of consumerism's positive assessment of it, it will be useful to set it against what is normally meant by style. Hopefully this will reveal the distinctiveness of the ideology of consumerism's position.

First we can acknowledge that most people will admit that image and style have become increasingly important for those who wield most power. The latter do, of course, exert the greatest influence in shaping the social contexts in which we live. There is, for example, ample evidence of a growing emphasis on corporate image. There is evidence, too, that employers are increasingly re-defining their skill requirements in terms of particular personality characteristics. More and more television time is given over to 'celebrities' whose main claim to fame is their 'in' image or style. And, as I have argued elsewhere, the trend in party politics and social policy is to privilege image over substance.[13]

There is little doubt that in important areas of life image and style are prominent. But while the examples cited above might suggest a 're-figuring of the social', this is not what the ideology of consumerism has in mind. The commonsense view suggests that the social influence of image and style derives from its use by those who wield power over the majority. The ideology of consumerism does not so much reject this view – it would be difficult to dispute it – but emphasises that individuals are capable of (and many do) subverting the images and style of the powerful. The re-figuring of the social is to be understood as a consequence of a *struggle* over style. For the ideology of consumerism this struggle can involve all consumers, but it is most evident in youth cultures.

Lury, in summarising studies of youth culture, notes that youth cultures are 'the sites of struggles over the control of meaning in a rapidly developing consumer culture, struggles played out in dress, demeanour, music and language'. Lury points out that the 'notion of resistance was central to ... early interpretations of youth sub cultures – style was seen as a form of defiance, political protest or semiotic guerrilla warfare'.[14]

Style, for the ideology of consumerism, since it is seen as part of the reshaping of the social, performs a political function, not just for the powerful, but importantly for the consumer. From a commonsense perspective it could be argued that the politics of style, and even the politics of culture, and identity, does not impact on society as profoundly and extensively as 'real' politics. Indeed to be sufficiently motivated to be engaged in 'struggles' over image and style is more suggestive of an apolitical self-preoccupation than a contestatory politics over matters of social significance. Even if advocates of the ideology of consumerism link the politics of style to something more approaching real politics, then this is surely a case of entering the land of absurdity. This might be the common-sense reaction to Paul Willis's statement that

> Even as 'the market' makes its profits, it supplies some of the materials for alternative or oppositional symbolic work. This is the

remarkable, unstable and ever unfolding contradiction of capitalism supplying materials for its own critique.[15]

While it might, at a stretch, be conceded that the politics of style is relevant for a politics of culture, to link it with a critique of capitalism, and by implication anti-capitalist politics, is nonsense. How can something as trivial as style be attributed with such political significance? How can what is essentially a matter of image and appearance be oppositional to capitalism? While not all advocates of the ideology of consumerism will be happy to agree with Willis, they do, nevertheless, make much of the cultural contradictions of capitalism and how these contradictions can be creatively exploited by the consumer in ways that contribute to the shaping of the social (via shaping consumer culture and culture in general) and in ways that contribute to self-actualisation.

The key to understanding the social significance that the ideology of consumerism attributes to style resides in its view that stylised consumption is part and parcel of the constitution and expression of self-identities. As we shall see, the ideology of consumerism views this in positive terms, and as such departs from the more common-sensical asessment of style in relation to self. A theoretical expression (and elaboration) of a common view is that offered by Stuart Ewen. For my purposes here it will be convenient briefly to consider the ways in which Ewen theorises the significance of commodification for self-identity.

Style and Self-alienation

The ideology of consumerism is quite happy to go along with Ewen's view that image, personality and style have become 'critical factor[s] in definitions of the self'.[16] Ewen's explanation for this, however, is totally unacceptable to the ideology of consumerism. He argues that the impact of industrial capitalism and urbanisation has effectively transformed the self. In the familiar tones of critical social theory, Ewen claims that the importance of character or inner self has been replaced by that of personality or outer self. This, he believes, can be understood in terms of the self's response to the new demands of relatively unskilled work requirements, and having to migrate from the familiarities of the closed community to an expanding urban context in which the individual has no roots and has to live as a stranger amongst strangers. In seeking employment, he argues, 'one knew how important it was to make a good "presentation". This new world required a sense of self that was malleable and sensitive to the power of the surface.'[17]

Similarly, 'Rooted in a past of patriarchal authority and arrangements between families, now relations of love, sexuality, and matrimony ... required new tools of negotiation.'[18] These new tools were those designed to craft style and image, and they were provided by the images of an expanding consumer culture.

> The emerging marketplace of consumer goods provided instruments for the construction of a self, to be seen, to be judged, to penetrate the wall of anonymity. In worlds of work and love, status and aspiration, the assembly of 'self' was becoming compulsory for ventures in society. The appeal of 'style' was not a matter of aesthetics alone; it was a functional acquisition of metropolitan life ... Style provided an extension of personality on a physical plane ...[19]

The little glimpse of Ewen's historical account of the emergence of the role of image and style in self-assembly is sufficient to render his thinking useless for the ideology of consumerism. He explicitly connects image and style with the surface, the outer self, the personality, the superficial and so on. Unlike contemporary advocates of the positive identity value of consumption, Ewen is not happy with the growing prominence of style, and he makes this abundantly clear.

> As frozen images – in ads or style magazines – become the models from which people design their living spaces or themselves, extreme alienation sets in. One becomes, by definition, increasingly uncomfortable in one's own skin. The constant availability of alternative styles to 'adapt to' thrives on this discomfort. The marketing engines of style depend on anomic subjects seeking to become splendid objects. The extent to which objects seem so promising may be but an index of the extent to which the human subject is in jeapordy; destined only to be defined as a consumer.[20]

The ideology of consumerism rejects this account for a number of reasons. First, Ewen's view represents an overly deterministic explanation of the power of advertisers over helpless consumers. He seems to be saying that consumers passively internalise the value that marketing professionals attribute to image and style as a consequence of the manipulative powers of advertisers. Against this view,, the ideology of consumerism emphasises the active and creative 'work' of consumers in matters of style. The language of manipulation has no place in the ideology of consumerism.

Second, Ewen seems to hold a narrow view of what is involved in stylised consumption, in which the images of advertisements (and style magazines) are the very images that penetrate the self. The self-relevance of image and style, for the ideology of consumerism, as we saw in the last chapter, cannot be restricted to *commodified* images and styles. On the contrary, styles are meaningfully created by individuals and subcultures out of *anything* at hand. The meanings that individuals invest in style creation reflect the *coherence* of the individual or subculture.

This connects with the third reason for the rejection of Ewen's view by the ideology of consumerism. Quite simply, Ewen's restricted conceptualisation of the meaning of style, and that com-modified images are 'forced' on to individuals, does lead him inevitably into positing self-alienation as an outcome of consumption. In other words Ewen is highly critical of the preoccupation with image and style, whereas, for the ideology of consumerism, it is a positive self-expressive undertaking. But for all the theoretical gymnastics dedicated to promoting the positive identity value of stylised consumption, the ideology of consumerism, as we shall see later, is unable to avoid the criticism that what it sees as self-expressive is nevertheless a form of self-alienation.

In many senses Ewen's views are representative of the kinds of ideas from which the latest ideology of consumerism has become well and truly distanced. The language of self-alienation, like that of manipulation, is not only regarded as too strong, but also, for the ideology of consumerism, it suggests a view of the 'ordinary' person that is far too demeaning for those committed to populism. Besides, the ideology of consumerism cannot countenance the possibility that the creative symbolic work which enables the consumer to assemble a positive self-identity is more appropriately understood as a manifestation of self-alienation. Somehow the language of creativity and free expression does not sit easily with the language of self-alienation.

There is a way out of this dilemma, but, as we shall see, it is as equally unappealing to the ideology of consumerism as Ewen's position. It is possible to argue (and Ewen does hint at this) that individuals are capable of 'putting on' a style (and 'taking it off') as befits particular circumstances. Thus a woman, for example, through choice of clothing, appearance, demeanour and speech, may 'put on' or construct a style that she thinks will create a good impression at a job interview. After getting the job she may modify her style, and she is most likely to discard it altogether in the confines of her home, and then put on another style for going out. She is likely to feel more at ease with herself when she adopts a style that is consistent with her self-identity, or dispenses altogether with any kind of style. Styles that are readily discarded tend to be those that are not part of her self-identity.

The above example illustrates something that is familiar: most people recognise that almost everybody is involved, to a greater or lesser degree, in what might be called 'strategic image-presentation' – social imperatives like getting a job and keeping it ensure this. It is something we do to adapt pragmatically to particular circumstances, especially so when in the company of those who are in a position to wield power over us. Obviously, people vary in their willingness and capacity 'to play this game'. But conceptualising the role of style or image for the self in this way avoids the pitfalls of attributing unwarranted manipulative powers to consumer culture. The consumer, consistent with the ideology of consumerism, is seen as a knowledgeable, autonomous agent in the sense that it is the individual who decides on the images and styles to be adopted and discarded. Also, in keeping with a tendency within the ideology of consumerism, strategic image-presentation can be used in both conformist and non-conformist ways.

Style as strategic image-presentation is neither necessarily inherently self-alienating, nor trivialising, of self-identity. Ewen's fears about self-alienation and about consumers becoming superficial persons need apply only to those who *permanently* become objects of style. The shop assistant's fake smile and artificial helpfulness might irritate but they are widely excused – being seen as a necessary part of the job. The person adopting the obliging shop assistant style may attempt to make the latter transparent by performing the role with an exaggerated enthusiasm, or by purposefully dropping the smile and so on.

Conceptualising style as a pragmatic strategy can allay Ewen's fears, and can be seen to be compatible with the ideology of consumerism's insistence on the individual's creative autonomy in the construction of style. However, style as a pragmatic strategy falls way short of what the ideology of consumerism means by 'style' and of the importance it attributes to style for self-identity. For the ideology of consumerism 'style' refers to something that is altogether more representative of *the self*. It is *the expression of self-identity*; it is both self-encompassing and self-engaging. In short, the reference is more akin to *lifestyle,* which may or may not involve active participation in one or more *style cultures.*

For the ideology of consumerism *lifestyle* is not something that one puts on and takes off. It is not an appendage of the self. It is something that is more or less continuously created throughout life. The coherence of a lifestyle reflects both the coherence of self-identity, and what is important to the self. This view does borrow much from early studies of youth subcultures. Commenting on these studies, Lury notes that

> ... what was seen to distinguish the activities of young people was the *internal coherence* of the style to which their creativity gave rise, the active articulation of objects with activities, expressions of belief and ways of life in a distinct ensemble. New meanings were seen to emerge as the elements of the style were combined into a unique whole or assemblage. This ensemble was seen to have its own internally generated unity in which dress, appearance, language, rituals, modes of interaction and genres of music gained their meaning in relation to one another. Each element of the style was seen to exist in a state of *homology* with every other.[21]

The earlier characterisation of the shop assistant, for the ideology of consumerism, misses the point. The real style of the shop assistant is most likely to be seen away from the confines of the work environment, in leisure activities. The latter allows a greater freedom of expression in terms of dress, appearance and cultural tastes. At work, glimpses of the style that is important to the individual may be displayed via culturally coded signs such as wearing rings through an eyebrow, black nail varnish, the use of a word that denotes familiarity with a particular subcultural style, or a slogan on a bag, for example.

For some advocates of the ideology of consumerism, theorising the identity value of consumption through considerations of style is too restrictive and dated: the subcultural styles of mods, rockers and punks, for example, which formed the basis of theorising stylised consumption, belonged to an earlier era. Too much can be made of self-identities as somehow reflecting the internal coherence of spectacular styles. Today, it is argued, there is a proliferation of rapidly emerging and fading styles and thus more 'scope for invention and adoption of ... new subjectivities'.[22] Such a view does play into the hands of those who are convinced that the ideology of consumerism, in stressing the positive identity value of consumption, is not in fact dealing with self-identity at all. To be able to talk of *adopting* subjectivities does suggest that the ideology of consumerism defines self-identity in 'throw-away' terms that reflect assumptions more appropriate to conceptualising image than self-identity.

One commonsense response to the ideology of consumerism's attribution of significance to style for self-identity may be that of pointing out that for all the fine talk about internal coherence, creativity, meaning, ensembles and homologies, it does not alter the fact that style relates more to image and appearance than to more substantial aspects of self and self-identity. We can say that basing the importance of style for self-identities on the internal coherence of the style is unconvincing. Trivia, after all, can be creatively assembled into a coherent form.

One is led to ask why it is that people should invest their creative energies in how they appear to others. Has style become so important to the self that individuals are becoming active (and creative) agents in their own trivialisation and self-alienation? The view that stylised consumption involves consumers in carefully and creatively making decisions to construct, maintain and display their self-identities does summon up images of self-preoccupied individuals pouring their energies into transforming their selves into insubstantial objects. The question arises: for whom is this true?

Empirical Questions

Most people recognise that what the ideology of consumerism means by style does have a certain relevance for youth. Adolescence is a period during which identity experimentation occurs. More specifically it is an intense period of self-discovery in which the individual's desire to exercise autonomy invariably encounters the constraining forces of authority and the demands of schooling. It is not surprising that in this context the individual may want to let the adult world know that he or she is 'coming of age'. One means of doing this is for the individual to assert his or her difference from the adults around them. And one of the most spectacular ways of doing this is to adopt a recognisable style that successfully expresses this difference. Recognisable styles, too, are signalling devices to others – those one wants to avoid and those one wants to associate with. In this respect the image of the style, appearance, mannerisms, musical tastes, use of language and so on, is important. In societies so thoroughly impregnated with the images of consumer culture it would be surprising if these images did not play a significant part in the *communication* of style. But it would be foolish to assume that these images constitute the self or are centrally involved in the construction of self-identity, other than temporarily.

What I am alluding to here is that there are crucial differences between the self, self-identity, image and style. The literature constituting the latest ideology of consumerism fails, for the most part, to observe these differences. Some of this failure may be unintentional – a product of sloppy and muddled thinking. If this is the case then it must be said that the academics responsible for this compare unfavourably with the 'ordinary person'. Parents, when faced with teenagers who have adopted a style that they find disagreeable, often remark that 'they will grow out of it', and they do. Adults who appear to be serious in adopting a style or who appear to pride themselves on using consumer goods to develop, maintain and display a particular lifestyle – perhaps in an effort to achieve status, or merely to express their difference – are often the objects of derision and ridicule. And it is more or less universally taken to be a criticism when a person is judged to be 'all style and no substance'. All of these examples suggest that people have little difficulty in distinguishing self and self-identity from image and style.

These examples, too, provide a kind of empirical evidence – the evidence of common perceptions – that is ignored by the ideology of consumerism. For all of the claims that the current theoretical consensus explaining consumption is rooted in the experience of ordinary people, we find nothing of the sort. The ethnographic studies that supposedly support the positive identity value of consumption are misleading for reasons discussed in the previous chapter. But, importantly here, and leaving aside potential distortions, the studies most commonly used are those of youth. Even if we generously admit that consumer culture positively benefits the quest for identity in youth, we have no grounds whatsoever to assume that the wider population benefits in the same, or even similar, ways. The ideology of consumerism, not only overgeneralises from the identity experiments of youth, but in mistaking image for identity, it contradicts the experiences of the vast majority.

Sources of Identity

Self-identities, according to the ideology of consumerism, are today almost exclusively formed and maintained via consumption. Indeed, according to Willis, 'commodities are all most people have'.[23] 'Having', it would seem, is the major source of self-identity! This is clearly absurd. Again it suggests a highly impoverished view of what self-identity is – all the more so when we remind ourselves that what we have is used for its symbolic value in self-assembly. The ideology of consumerism quite understandably focuses on consumption to the exclusion of all else. The inevitable consequence of this is that other sources of meaning, of pleasure and of self-identity are ignored. This is obviously a recipe for the production of distorted and inflated claims. What is ignored may well be more important sources of self-identity than either consumer products or the images of consumer culture.

Are we seriously to believe that the images of consumer culture, or indeed the individualised meanings that we attribute to the objects of consumption, override the influence of parents, friends, significant role models and so on? Are self-identities devoid of any of the influences of early socialisation, or of the range of experiences that life throws up, or of our experiences of success and failure, satisfaction and emptiness, and so on?

Now, the ideology of consumerism avoids these kinds of questions. It prefers to emphasise the growing and all-pervasive presence of consumer culture and that experiences today are (mass-)mediated. Of course there is much truth in this. The private spaces of the home are pieced together and embellished with consumer products. Television invades the home with adverts, and thus the context of our more intimate experiences. Does this mean that the images of consumer culture become the building-blocks of our self-identities? Do our experiences and activities other than those mediated by consumer culture count for nothing? If a young boy's self-identity is largely based on his footballing skill – not that unusual – how are we to explain this in terms of consumer culture? Is the televisual lure of a high-profile footballer's lavish lifestyle to be deemed more influential than the supportive attentions of parents, teachers or a neighbour, or the positive recognition from peers, or the experiences of excitement and exhilaration he derives from playing football?

This example not only highlights the fact that the most influential sources of self-identity arise from our interactions with people important to us, but that those self-identities that revolve around what the individual likes *doing* best involve, for their development and maintenance, the opportunities, time and considerable effort on the part of the individual. In other words these self-identities involve a self-expressive form of *material autonomous action*. Of course some of the resources required to enable such action may come in the form of consumer products – a person who best expresses himself or herself through the exercise of DIY skills does need to purchase tools. In this case the tools have a material use value (rather than symbolic value) in relation to the person's self-identity. It is impossible to see the relevance of the images of consumer culture for such a self-identity, or indeed any self-identity involving a self-expressive autonomy not centred on self-image.

Self-identities involve much more than appearance, self-image and style. Self-identity is that part of the self that is most important and most authentic to the person. It is the repository of enduring feelings about oneself, and it is these feelings that materialise in interests, ambitions and aspirations. It is these feelings, too, that determine self-relevant meanings. Understood in this way it is well nigh impossible to see the relevance of consumer culture for the more important and substantial aspects of self-identity.

The Image Industry

But what of the significance of consumer culture for those aspects of self-identity – body, appearance, image – that are exclusively the province of the ideology of consumerism? There is no doubt that consumer culture is centrally relevant here. It would also seem to be the case, especially among young people, that appearance is of considerable importance. The body, too, has, for increasing numbers of young and older people, become a site to be 'worked on'. For older people, at least, concern with the body would seem to be more for reasons of health than image. Nevertheless, even older people are not immune from preoccupations with image.

As we have seen, the ideology of consumerism, especially in its theorisation of style, not only views a preoccupation with image as positive, but emphasises the positive role of consumer objects and culture in stylised consumption. In doing this the ideology of consumerism distances itself from those accounts of the influence of consumer culture that seem to rule out the potential that exists for the consumer to engage creatively in so-called symbolic work. Yet there is a 'downside' to the interventions of consumer culture into self-identity matters.

Advertising has played no small part in promoting the view, for example, that to be a woman is to be a body. But, more than this, it promotes a particular kind of body as attractive, and in so doing is implicated in the increase in anorexia and the attendant eating disorders. The images of consumer culture may well be used positively by many individuals involved in the 'symbolic labour' of image construction, but this does not justify being upbeat about something that is experienced by many in more negative terms. While the ideology of consumerism laudably wants to dispense with any hint of an idea that the consumer is manipulated by consumer culture, are we to rule out this possibility altogether?

I am not about to resurrect the discredited argument that advertisers manipulate and deceive an unsuspecting public and that as a consequence the consumer is well and truly duped. I shall argue, however, that advertisers do *attempt to manipulate and deceive* and that these attempts *may be effective* on the most vulnerable. Amongst the most vulnerable I include the older pre-teens, youth (including those represented in the youth studies referred to earlier) and those with a fragile self-identity. It is these people who are most likely to be influenced, directly or indirectly through friends and peers, by the relentless forces that attempt to commodify self-image.

There can be no disputing the fact that advertisers attempt to cash in on what is widely recognised as a growing preoccupation with self-identity. In truth self-identity cannot be commodified. But what advertisers do is *translate* genuine concerns pertaining to self-identity into a form that can be addressed by the purchase of commodities. In this translation the original identity problem becomes something other than it is, and remains. Self-confidence, for example, can take a battering from all sorts of normal experiences – loss of love, marriage break-up, loss of a job, not being taken seriously by significant others, and so on. A series of such experiences may result in chronic feelings of anxiety, which in some may connect with a fundamental sense of insecurity. The need for 'ontological security', as Ronald Laing referred to it,[24] can be met only through experiencing an unconditional acceptance of oneself in enduring relationships. Ontological security is the basis of genuine self-confidence.

Advertisers can no more sell genuine self-confidence than they can sell ontological security. Neither can be bought or sold. Rather, advertisers sell images. Images, being images, are totally irrelevant to identity-needs. Continuing our example, a common advertising technique is to align images of self-confidence with images of success – success in a job, in getting a partner, being popular and so forth. Of course, these images converge in the particular product on offer. A person's lack of self-confidence, and maybe lack of ontological security, are thus translated into the 'need' for certain products. The implication here is that by buying a particular product the problems of insecurity and lack of self-confidence will be solved. While this is obviously a false solution, and while people know this, the least knowledgeable and the most vulnerable and desperate may actually try the products 'just in case'.

The above example may go some way toward explaining why useless items of clothing are purchased, why some women, who know better, buy anti-ageing, anti-wrinkle and anti-cellulite creams, and why 'prestige' brands find enough customers to warrant their prestige prices. But the example does also illustrate that *the identity value of consumption is restricted to self-image* and that *this can take a negative form.*

As Anthony Giddens points out, 'The consumption of ever-novel goods becomes in some part a substitute for the genuine development of self; appearance replaces essence ...'.[25] He goes on to use Zygmunt Bauman's argument to elaborate this view, in a way that recalls Ewen's warnings of the self-alienating consequences of consumption.

> Individual needs of personal autonomy, self-definition, authentic life or personal perfection are all translated into the need to possess, and consume, market-offered goods. This translation, however, pertains to the *appearance* [my emphasis] of use value of such goods, rather than to the use value itself; as such it is intrinsically inadequate and ultimately self-defeating, leading to momentary assuagement of desires and lasting frustration of needs ...[26]

While both Giddens and Bauman in my view over-estimate the numbers of people manipulated by the forces of commodification (Bauman refers to 'the seduced' as constituting approximately two-thirds of the populations of the more affluent societies),[27] they nevertheless provide credible accounts of how advertisers work *on the most vulnerable.* Bearing my proviso in mind, Bauman is surely correct when he argues that 'The market feeds on the unhappiness it generates: the fears, anxieties and the sufferings of personal inadequacy it induces releases the consumer behaviour indispensable to its continuation.'[28]

Giddens, commenting on Bauman's argument, notes that 'Commodification is in some ways even more insidious than this characterisation suggests. For the project of the self as such may become heavily commodified. Not just lifestyles, but self-actualisation is packaged and distributed according to market criteria.'[29]

Choosing Self-identity

The inadequacies of the ideology of consumerism's theorisation of the identity value of consumption can be detailed as follows: first, it replaces self-identity with self-image and in the process trivialises the concept of self-identity. Second, by over-generalising from the identity experiments of youth it exaggerates the extent to which we are all preoccupied with image and style. Third, by ignoring sources of self-identity other than those provided by consumer culture it exaggerates the importance of consumer culture for self-identity. Fourth, it provides a distorted account of the value of consumer culture for self-identity by focusing solely on the alleged benefits for the individual. These alleged benefits are more appropriately seen as self-alienating, and for the most vulnerable can be experienced as highly negative.

From the viewpoint of the ideology of consumerism all of these criticisms are unjustified and are rendered irrelevant by virtue of failing to take into consideration the significance of choice for the individual consumer. In this regard the ideology of consumerism, it must be said, is at one with what has become a truism in recent thinking about self-identity. Thus Giddens, who is no friend of consumer culture, not only acknowledges that choices reflect self-identity, but tells us that 'lifestyle choice is increasingly important in the constitution of self-identity ...'.[30] More than this, 'in conditions of high modernity, we all not only follow lifestyles, but in an important sense are forced to do so – we have no choice but to choose'.[31] So there you have it – *everybody has to choose*, *everybody* (not just youth) makes consumer choices, and through these choices *everybody chooses their self-identity*. Giddens also tells us that

In the post-traditional order of modernity, and against the backdrop of new forms of mediated experience, self-identity becomes a reflexively organised endeavour. The reflexive *project* [my emphasis] of the self, which consists in the sustaining of coherent, *yet continuously revised* [my emphasis], biographical narratives, takes place in the context of multiple choice.[32]

In the hands of the ideology of consumerism, in spite of Giddens's warning that his notion of lifestyle should not be mistaken for a superficial consumerism, these statements provide ample justification for what is in fact a consumerist-centred account of self-identity. Be that as it may, the specific point that I want to make here is that such statements, far from absolving the ideology of consumerism from the criticisms made against it, actually reinforce those criticisms. First, Giddens and the ideology of consumerism wrongly identify *the* identity problem as that of *finding* and *choosing* a self-identity. We all have self-identities. The real identity problem, as mental health statistics reveal, is that of developing and maintaining a *meaningful and satisfying identity*.[33]

To be fair to Giddens he does recognise this both in his reference to the need for a coherent self-identity and in understanding this in relation to the need for ontological security, authenticity and self-actualisation, amongst other things. But whereas Giddens attempts to balance the need for coherence with that of continuously revising self-identity through choice, the ideology of consumerism privileges continuous choice and revision to the neglect of the more enduring and stabilising influences on the self. As a consequence self-identity is conceptualised as forever chosen anew, that is, as temporary, transient, fluid and thus tending toward the trivial and superficial. As Christopher Lasch argues:

> The idea that 'you can be anything you want' … has come to mean that identities can be adopted and discarded like a change of costume … But if choice no longer implies commitments and consequences … the freedom to choose amounts in practice to an abstention of choice.[34]

As we shall see in the next chapter, the freedom to choose one's self-identity, in the hands of the ideology of consumerism, is a crucial element in the promotion of consumption as a realm of freedom.

4　Consumption as Freedom

We have already encountered a number of ways in which the ideology of consumerism associates consumption with freedom. The current theoretical descriptions and explanations of consumption are full of references to consumption as an arena of choice, in which individuals make lifestyle choices, choose self-identities, play with meaning, seek pleasures and so on. I have noted how this kind of view has developed in sharp contrast to those views that emphasised mass, standardised, consumption-evoking conformity among the masses in terms of aspirations and mind-sets. Rather than a passive conformity, consumer culture is now widely believed to encourage an active, creative engagement in the pursuit of difference and individuality. Passivity and conformity suggest unfreedom. Creative activity and individuality suggest freedom. It can be agreed with Bauman that for the latest ideology of consumerism consumption is 'firmly established as the focus, and the playground, for individual freedom'.[1]

That individuals do possess capacities for autonomous action will not be disputed. Indeed this assumption is central to the theory of consumption to be developed in Part Two of this book. And in Part Three, I shall argue that the expansion of the realm of autonomy enabling the development of capacities for autonomy, and autonomous action, are crucial both for the well-being of the individual and the planet. However, I will take issue with the ideology of consumerism's conceptualisation of autonomy. Essentially I shall argue that it is a severely limited autonomy – a confined autonomy that does not add up to much. It adds up to so little that it hardly qualifies as autonomy or freedom at all. This does not mean that I am resurrecting the myth of the passive, duped consumer. The consumer, it can be acknowledged, is, amongst other things, active and creative. It is doubtful, however, that this is the best way to characterise the consumer. I will argue, borrowing a phrase from André Gorz, that the consumer is more appropriately conceptualised as engaging in a form of 'active passivity'.

The claim that the realm of consumption has become a realm of freedom is based on a number of ideas. As we have seen in previous chapters much is made of the fact that the individual is a meaning-maker, and that this is the source of the individual's freedom. Why the freedom to create meaning should be focused on consumption is never made clear. Anyway, this interpretive freedom, for the ideology of consumerism, develops in interaction with the material and symbolic resources of consumer culture. This interaction, significantly for the ideology of consumerism, facilitates the choosing of self-identity. Consumer culture, it is thus maintained, enhances the very freedom of the individual.

Rather than re-state my criticisms of these views I will be more concerned, in this chapter, to indicate that their limitations and misleading nature arise primarily from what the ideology of consumerism ignores. In particular, I shall argue that an exclusive focus on the little ways in which it might be said that consumption is a realm of freedom to the neglect of rather obvious ways in which it clearly is not, does promote the myth of consumer freedom. Crucial here will be considerations of the fact that participation in consumption involves *dependence* on employment. The latter is increasingly insecure, meaningless and anything but free. I shall also argue that *consumption, rather than being an arena of freedom, constitutes a field of dependence by virtue of the alienation of labour.*

The ideology of consumerism considers these kinds of criticisms to be ill-founded. The freedom of the consumer is articulated in ways that are intended to render dependence on employment irrelevant. And the view that consumption is a field of dependence, rather than freedom, as an inevitable consequence of the alienation of labour, is regarded as dated. In adopting this view, the ideology of consumerism emphasises the freedom-enhancing properties of choice. It will thus be necessary to examine critically the role of choice for the ideology of consumerism. My main argument here will be that *consumer choice gives a semblance of freedom only,* and that *it actually reinforces the negation of freedom.*

Finally, I shall return to a theme that was broached in the Introduction to this book: that of basic needs. I argued that one of the main reasons why the theoretical consensus on consumption has developed into an uncritical form is that it has dispensed with any notion of need. The significance of a theory of needs for a theory of consumption will be made apparent in Part Two. In this chapter, however, I will argue that in removing needs from consideration, the ideology of consumerism is able falsely to promote consumption as indicative of freedom – viewing consumption as symbolic is important here. This contributes immensely to the myth of affluence that is so dear to free market ideology.

Throughout this chapter it will be appropriate to draw out the similarities and differences between the ideology of consumerism and free market ideology. Consumption as the main arena for individual freedom is one of the platforms of the ideologies generated in the promotion of free market capitalism. The ideology of consumerism suffers an ambiguous relationship with free market capitalism. Nowhere is this relationship more difficult than on the issue of consumer freedom. Among the advocates of the latest ideology of consumerism there are those who want to distance themselves from free market ideology, a few who embrace it and the vast majority who ignore it by observing a disturbing silence. In commenting on the work of Paul Willis, Jim McGuigan notes 'his faith in market capitalism's capacity to deliver the goods for everyone's creative use'. McGuigan mentions Willis's reference 'to the gulf between Left intellectuals and ordinary people and, moreover, the manifest failure of socialism in the late twentieth century'. McGuigan comments:

> The aim, therefore, is clearly to challenge worn-out radical assumptions rather than worn-out conservative ones. In consequence, Willis has nowhere else to look than to the unqualified pleasures of consumer sovereignty in the marketplace. At best this is a libertarian humanism of uncertain political provenance, at worst it signals a loss of conviction in any grounds for criticising what exists in a world where human happiness does not seem wholly ubiquitous and where, apparently, there is no compelling vision of a better future.[2]

Thus, prior to examining critically the assumptions that enable the ideology of consumerism to celebrate consumption as a realm of freedom, it will be necessary to clarify its relationship with free market ideology.

Capitalism, Freedom, Consumption

André Gorz refers to 'the neo-liberal credo that all problems are best resolved by allowing free rein to the laws of the market'.[3] Part of this credo is the promise of greater prosperity for everyone. The freedom of the market, by generating greater prosperity, enables individual freedom. We express this freedom in consumption, particularly in the consumer choices that we make. Or, if you like, all problems which the individual encounters can be solved by expanding, via the 'free market', his or her freedom to consume. This is the supposed pay-off, available to all individuals, for encouraging the freedom of the wealth-creators freely to do what they do best.

Of course, in practice, the market is anything but free – its laws are determined by the most powerful transnational corporations whose primary allegiance is to major investors. The big transnational companies are aided and abetted by what is, in effect, a world government – what Gorz describes as a 'supra-national state' comprising the WTO (World Trade Orgaization), the IMF (International Monetary Fund), the World Bank, the OECD (Organization for Economic and Cooperative Development) and US military power (sometimes in the guise of NATO). For reasons that will become clear, I see neo-liberal credo as part of a broader ideology – an imperialist new right ideology.

The consequences of the implementation of this ideology, which is essentially about the freedom to make profit, are devastating for the overwhelming majority of the world's population and for the planet. We have known this for some time. It has long been established that whatever temporary consumer benefits a minority might enjoy from capitalism, the vast majority are denied a full life, physically, socially and emotionally. A recent report of the United Nations Development Programme, cited by Bauman, includes a number of familiar statistics.

1 billion people 'cannot satisfy even their elementary needs'. Among 4.5 billion of the residents of the 'developing' countries, three in every five are deprived access to basic infrastructures: a third have no access to drinkable water, a quarter have no accommodation worthy of its name, one-fifth have no use of sanitary and medical services. One in five children spend less than five years in any form of schooling; a similar proportion is permanently undernourished.[4]

Now, no doubt I will be accused of being simplistic in stating that capitalism is *the cause* of all of this. Sure enough capitalism does its work on ground already fouled by colonialism, imperialism, corruption and tradition. But in the final analysis it is the relentless pursuit of ever more obscene profits that is the ultimate and underlying cause. We have known this for some time too. Marx knew it and proved it; André Gunder Frank updated Marx in the light of the development of capitalism, and Frank's theory requires elaboration only in order to accommodate more recent developments.[5] It is the more recent developments that have caused a widening of the gap between rich and poor.

In the United Nations report, mentioned above, some interesting statistics chart the uneven impact of capitalism. The 'global consumption of goods and services was twice as big in 1997 as in 1975 and had multiplied by a factor of six since 1950'. Yet in 'seventy to eighty of the hundred or so "developing" countries the average income per head of the population is today lower than ten or even thirty years ago: 120 million people live on less than one dollar a day'.[6]

Statistical information of this sort is abundantly available and contradicts the promise of consumer freedom as a universal outcome of wealth-creation. It does more than this. It conclusively indicates that the life-threatening consequences of capitalism, for the majority of the world's population, are far more extensive than anything that can be achieved via means of terror. And, as with national governments of a new right persuasion, the 'world government' *knows* this to be the case.

In a leaked internal memo, a World Bank vice-president displays a disregard for the lives of potential victims of policies – the transfer of high-polluting industries from the more affluent societies to the Third World – that he advocates the Bank should promote. He suggests that 'health impairing pollution should be done in the country with the lowest cost, which will be the country with the lowest wages ...'. For the Bank, 'the economic logic behind dumping a load of toxic waste in the lowest wage country is impeccable and we should face up to that'. This logic is spelled out to justify what might more appropriately represent an intent to murder, conduct genocide or engage in international terrorism.

I've always thought that underpopulated countries in Africa are vastly under-polluted, their air quality is probably vastly inefficiently high compared to Los Angeles or Mexico City ... Concern over an agent that causes one in a million chance of prostate cancer is obviously going to be much higher in a country where people survive to get prostate cancer than in a country where under-5 mortality is 200 per thousand.[7]

It is precisely because those who are most responsible for promoting free market ideology *know* that it is a fiction, *know* that unfettered capitalism is by far and away the most significant cause of premature deaths, yet coerce all governments to acquiesce to the laws of free market capitalism, that I prefer to refer to this particular ideology as new right ideology, rather than neo-liberal ideology. Consumer freedom in new right ideology, in reality, can be achieved only for a minority at the expense of the majority.

To most readers the New Right will be associated with right-wing governments hell bent on opening up society by de-regulation to free market forces and by repressive legislation to criminalise potential opposition to the disorder created. The disorder in question is that of dismantling the safety-net of the welfare state, the privat-isation of publicly owned industries and services, and the undermining of employees' rights. And, of course, all of this is done in the name of democracy, freedom and consumer freedom.

While the latest ideology of consumerism dovetails rather neatly with the New Right's promotion of consumer sovereignty, it is a mistake to conflate the two. The ideology of consumerism has its roots in Cultural Studies and has developed against the backdrop of opposition to the Cultural Establishment, and disputes within the academic left. Sure enough in the 1980s some of these disputes revolved around how best to interpret the cultural dimensions of new right 'social' policy. For most Cultural Studies academics, new right ideology was, and still is, a poisonous, simplistic nonsense. In spite of its glaring errors, the ideology of consumerism is far more sophisticated than any discourse ever produced by right-wing thought – a contradiction in terms if ever there was one.

For the New Right, consumer sovereignty is promoted almost entirely in terms of its alleged economic advantages, that is, in terms of exchange value and use value. For the ideology of consumerism, economics is irrelevant. As we shall see this enables the ideology of consumerism shamefully to ignore the fictions of new right ideology and the effects of its implementation. In promoting consumer freedom for its symbolic and identity value the ideology of con-sumerism inadvertently supports the reproduction of inequalities on a global and national scale.

Both new right ideology and the ideology of consumerism base their respective notions of consumer sovereignty on the expansion of choice – more choice equates with more freedom, both define freedom itself in terms of consumption, and both articulate freedom solely in terms of the freedom or autonomy of *the individual* – there is an absence of any notion of collective freedom or autonomy. Freedom has, in both ideologies, become privatised. As Bauman correctly observes, 'The freedom of mankind has been translated as the freedom of every one of its individual members.'[8] This alone, I shall argue below, produces a loss of freedom.

Freedom as Unfreedom

The privatisation of freedom, for both new right ideology and the ideology of consumerism, refers to the conceptualisation of freedom in terms of consumer choices.[In the ideology of consumerism, consumer choices reflect the interpretive freedom of the individual, and this is increasingly understood as a freedom that is harnessed to the project of creating a self-identity.]For the New Right the privat-isation of freedom also refers, amongst other things, to the privatisation of hitherto publicly provided, or heavily subsidised, collective facilities, resources and services that were available for everybody. Here privatisation means replacing state provision with several competing service providers, and this alone is supposed to give the consumer more choice. But there is more freedom to come. State-provided services and facilities are paid for out of taxation on individual incomes. When the state no longer provides, so the story goes, it can reduce the tax burden on individuals, thereby enabling individuals to have more money in their pockets. The extra money now enables individuals the freedom to choose the services and facilities they want.

On the face of it economic privatisation and the consumer freedom it is supposed to support has absolutely nothing to do with the consumer freedom celebrated by the ideology of consumerism. However, I shall argue that the ideology of consumerism does its work, so to speak, in ways that confirm the loss of freedom produced by the materialisation of new right privatisation policies.

Experience of economic privatisation has borne out the fact that it generates social inequalities, insecurities and, importantly, a loss of freedom. The 'common good' was predicated on the principle of equal access to security and freedom-enabling resources. The New Right's obsession with privatisation is intended to replace the common good with consumption by private individuals. As a consumer, Gorz noted prior to the privatisation initiatives of recent decades, 'the individual is encouraged ... to reconstitute himself as a *private* microcosm which he can enjoy and over which he can reign as solitary sovereign'.[9] The privatisation of 'the common good', in practice, 'is to *constrain* [my emphasis] the individual to buy back individually, as a consumer, the means of satisfaction of which the society has socially deprived him'.[10] More recently Bauman graphically comments that:

> The big banknote has been exchanged for a barrelful of coppers, so that all individuals may carry some coins in their pockets. And they would be wise to do so and to dig, if needed, into their own pockets – since the large-denomination bill once kept in the collective trust of the species and guaranteeing the solvency of each one and all together is no longer in the safe.[11]

So what the New Right promotes as the expansion of freedom is actually a loss of freedom. As Noam Chomsky puts it: 'All this talk about capitalism and freedom has got to be a conscious fraud. As soon as you move into the real world, you see that nobody could actually believe that nonsense.'[12] In the real world no amount of private consumer freedom can compensate for the loss of freedom brought about by the destruction of the common good. The ideology of consumer freedom, caught up as it is in viewing freedom as the freedom of the private individual, cannot conceptualise the freedom located in the common good. It thus has nothing to say about the disappearance of this freedom, and this does constitute a serious omission in the ideology of consumerism's concept of freedom.

It can be argued, from the viewpoint of the ideology of consumerism, that this omission is nowhere near as serious as I am suggesting. It is evident that, in practice, the New Right's concept of freedom is based on the money available to the individual. For the more sophisticated ideology of consumerism this will not do. To make money the currency of freedom suggests a highly crude and impoverished concept of freedom. Laudably the ideology of consumerism wants to avoid this. But, rather than being informed by a comprehensive theory of freedom, the ideology of consumerism emphasises that freedom resides in the individual to the exclusion of all other considerations, such as access to material resources, the social structuration of opportunities, asymmetries of social power and so on. Indeed, the freedom of the individual is itself reduced to an interpretive freedom as if this is sufficient to explain the freedom *to act*. But, even if we acknowledge that the ideology of consumerism embraces a radically different concept of freedom from that of new right ideology, we may still want to ask how it deals with the loss of freedom brought about by a disappearing common good. The answer remains: it does not.

Reducing freedom to money is certainly crude, yet it contains a truth in a crude world. In distancing itself from this banal truth, the ideology of consumerism distances itself from the real world in which money has become the main currency of freedom. Consequently the ideology of consumerism's concept of freedom has very little relevance to the real world. More than this, however, what it asserts as freedom does perform an ideological function far more successfully than new right ideology in so far as it better conceals (at an ideological level if not in reality) the social inequalities and unfreedoms which characterise the world and societies that we inhabit.

Freedom within Dependence

Even though the ideology of consumerism acknowledges that people do buy goods – how could it not? – the freedom of the consumer is not located in the freedom to buy, but in how the consumer interacts with what is bought and/or with the images of consumer culture. In approaching the freedom of the consumer in this way, it is presumed that the ideology of consumerism avoids vulnerability to the criticisms levelled against the New Right's ideology of consumer sovereignty. This is true in the case of consumer freedom being understood as the creative symbolic labour involved in working with and working on the *images* of consumer culture. But, as we shall see later, the avoidance of one set of criticisms offers no protection from another, equally damaging, set of criticisms. However, in the case of consumer freedom being understood as the creative symbolic labour involved in working with and on *material* consumer products, the weaknesses of new right ideology are also present in the ideology of consumerism.

The most obvious weakness – perhaps the ideology of consumerism considers it is too obvious to mention – is that the free, creative use of material goods implies the purchase of goods. Quite simply this kind of freedom *is dependent on money*. Of course money is not freely and equally available to everyone, which already suggests that the ideology of consumer freedom, at least in its new right version, is a lie – some are more free than others. But more important here, money for the vast majority is earned. Consumer freedom is thus based on earned income and this in turn is *dependent* on being employed. Dependence, of course, is the opposite of autonomy or freedom. In a fundamental sense the freedom of the consumer is based on unfreedom. At best it is a freedom *within* dependence, that is a freedom within unfreedom. In emphasising consumption as the principal site of freedom, the ideology of consumerism may be silently acknowledging that other areas of life, such as work, for example, do not offer comparable freedoms, but it does not tell us that consumption is a limited sphere of freedom dependent on unfreedom.

It is no surprise that new right propaganda equating freedom with consumer freedom goes into overdrive during periods in which secure employment becomes scarce. The propaganda slows down as it becomes clear that a new normality is in place and that people have adapted to it. And so it is today that the unfreedom underpinning consumer freedom *forces* almost everybody into a dependence on uncertain employment, that is into a dependence on the undependable. Uncertain employment spells an uncertain future. This is a recipe for inducing anxiety – all the more so given the dismantling of the common good.

The emphasis on consumer freedom within the ideology of consumerism deflects attention away from the unfreedom rooted in our dependence on the undependable in order to participate in the arena of freedom. In this sense it colludes with new right ideology. It also deflects attention away from the consequences of new policies, which new right ideology, however vigorous in its efforts, fails to conceal – insecure dependence, structural unemployment, poverty and increasing social inequality. In this sense the latest ideology of consumerism is an extension of new right ideology.

This extension achieves its fullest development from that part of the ideology of consumerism that considers itself immune to the criticisms outlined above. I am referring to that conceptualisation of freedom that emphasises the freedom of the individual to engage in creative symbolic labour on the *images of consumer culture*. In a sense the ideology of consumerism is saying: 'You don't need money to be free and to freely express yourself. Images are free, and they are freely supplied by consumer culture in abundance. You are free to do with them what you will.' Lack of money may prevent the individual from purchasing commodities, but it does not bar a full and free participation with the images of consumer culture. I shall have more to say about this version of freedom later. For the moment, however, it can be noted that the freedom-undermining effects of new right policies are not only ignored, they no longer constitute problems. A lack of money can be more than adequately compensated by creative symbolic labour. Being dependent on insecure employment is no longer a problem – in fact, the time made available in periods of unemployment can be a blessing. Unemployment, after all, releases time for creative symbolic labour! Inequalities generated by the unequal distribution of income, alone, are no longer a problem. Indeed, the language of social inequalities is replaced by the language of differences. The latter, of course, is more suited to capturing the benefits of consumer culture for providing an arena in which free individuals create and express their stylised self-identities.

A symbolic freedom, based as it is on interpretive freedom, is, as I shall argue later, an inconsequential freedom. But what of the realm of material consumption as an arena of freedom? I have already argued that whatever freedom this arena offers, it is a freedom based on unfreedom, by virtue of the fact that to participate in it requires dependence on an income. As individuals we can all appreciate this fact. But the original source of our (collective) loss of freedom – *we* are not free not to sell our labour time – resides in the alienation of labour.

I am not referring to self-alienation (although the alienation of labour produces self-alienation in employment), I am referring to the fact that under the dominance of capitalism we (labour) do not determine what is produced. Labour, both manual and mental, is put in the service of capitalism. The world of consumer goods is thus produced by alienated, that is unfree, labour. And, it is because we no longer produce what we consume, or consume what we produce (that is, because we are not in control of producing for our basic needs) that these needs can be satisfied only by the purchase of goods produced by others. To satisfy our survival needs we are *not free not to buy* the relevant goods. In the same way that it is perverse to refer to workers' autonomy within the alienation of labour, so too is it perverse to refer to the realm of consumption as a realm of freedom when participation in this realm is a requirement, a necessity. Whatever freedoms accrue in the realm of consumption, they are freedoms within unfreedom, and reflect our powerlessness to act otherwise.

Some advocates of the latest ideology of consumerism may acknowledge that under capitalism labour is alienated, that some degree of alienation in employment is inevitable, that employment has become increasingly insecure, and that all of this adds up to a lack of freedom. But whereas I have argued that this lack of freedom manifests itself as dependence, concretely dependence on employment for income, in order to participate in consumption, the latest ideology of consumerism prefers to see consumption as a realm of freedom in sharp contrast to employment as a sphere of unfreedom. In other words, the ideology of consumerism does not view consumption as a realm dependent on unfreedom, but rather as one that is *the* alternative to unfreedom. (This is consistent with the tendency in Cultural Studies to theorise culture as an autonomous entity without reference to politics and economics. It also begs the questions: Is there not more to life than work and consumption? Why should consumption be *the* alternative to work?) Indeed, for the ideology of consumerism, it is precisely because employment is a realm of limited opportunities for self-expression that consumption has become more prominent as a realm of freedom. Our dependence on employment is forgotten, and our dependence on consumer goods does not figure in the reckoning. Having cast aside our unfreedoms as irrelevant, all that is left for the ideology of consumerism to do is to spell out the ways in which consumption can be said to be a realm of freedom.

There are two major consequences of this manoeuver. First, the freedoms of consumption are inevitably exaggerated. Second, ignoring the fact that consumption is dependent on income, the ideology of consumerism displays an insensitivity to social inequalities and their impact on experience. As with new right ideology, some are more free than others. This is damaging to the universalistic claims of the ideology of consumerism. Recognition that this is so steers the ideology toward justifying its universal relevance by recourse to an emphasis on interpretive or symbolic freedom. This, of course, represents a drift away from a substantial (material) conception of freedom toward an insubstantial, largely inconsequential and trivial conception. Consumption as a realm of freedom is not only exaggerated, but the freedoms in question are trivial.

It is in this context that we can assess the validity of the claim, advanced by both new right ideology and the ideology of consumerism, that our freedoms in consumption have increased as a consequence of the growth of choices available in the realm of consumption. As we have seen in previous chapters, it is widely argued by both advocates and critics of the ideology of consumerism that today we are presented with a plurality of choices, both in consumption and self-identity, and that this very plurality of choice denotes a freedom that did not exist in earlier times.

It would be foolish to deny that the increasing proliferation of goods alone does mean that the consumer is faced with an ever expanding array of choices. But does this automatically translate into greater freedom? In what follows I shall argue that consumer choice, as it is understood by both new right ideology and the ideology of consumerism, cannot be unproblematically equated with freedom. And, in the ideology of consumerism, consumer choice, for the most part, amounts to a negation of freedom.

Freedom of Choice as Freedom

In the previous chapter, in assessing the identity value of consumption, it was argued that if the choices we make are inconsequential then, by definition, they are insignificant, both socially and to the self. It is highly misleading to somehow equate inconsequential choices with freedom. In ignoring the inconsequentiality of the choices on offer, the ideology of consumerism is, in fact, inadvertently claiming that the realm of consumption is a realm of trivial freedom. Christopher Lasch puts it thus:

> Unless the idea of choice carries with it the possibility of making a difference, of changing the course of events, of setting in motion a chain of events that may prove irreversible, it negates the freedom it claims to uphold. Freedom comes down to the freedom to choose between Brand X and Brand Y ...[13]

Following on from Lasch, a consequential choice might be viewed as one that makes a difference. Consequential choices evoke a concept of freedom consistent with the kind of significance attributed to freedom throughout the history of philosophy. By implication, the ideology of consumerism places itself outside of this tradition while misleadingly trying to hang on to its gravity.

This is not to say that all consumer choices are inconsequential. Many products are purchased precisely because it is anticipated that they will make a difference. For most people, 'making a difference' is understood in terms of an improvement on what was, whether it be a better television picture, better listening, more reliable or more comfortable driving, shoes that don't leak, a more comfortable house and so on. Purchases that 'make a difference' tend to be the 'one-off' or major (and thus, for most people, infrequent) purchase. Interestingly, and contrary to what we are led to believe by the ideology of consumerism, 'making a difference' tends to refer almost entirely to the use value of a commodity. For the ideology of consumerism, in sharp contrast, 'making a difference' is understood as making a symbolic difference, and increasingly as a symbolic difference constituting and better expressing style or image, themselves inconsequential for all but a vulnerable minority.

Making a choice that makes a difference is the exercise of a freedom or autonomy sufficiently powerful to make the difference in question. Consequential choices are thus choices reflecting some degree of power. The more our choices signify a substantial freedom, the greater the power enabling them. To be able to make a *material* difference, as is the intention in making the useful purchase, suggests a far more powerful consequence of choice than is the case with making a symbolic difference.

Those who attribute enormous significance to the symbolic will no doubt scoff at this. They will be able to cite numerous spectacular examples of the power of the symbolic – the fears experienced by Jewish people at the sight of a swastika; the rage experienced by Afro-Americans at the display of the Confederate flag; the delay in the peace process in the north of Ireland over what to name a future police force, and so on. But these examples, and others like them, do not signify the power of the symbolic, but rather the symbolisation of power or, more accurately, the symbolisation of the abuse of power. Making a symbolic difference appears to be consequential only when it represents the power responsible for actually making the difference in question.

The inconsequentiality of consumer choice derives from the powerlessness of the individual to make a difference. As I shall argue shortly our freedom to make consequential choices is limited in some obvious ways. But first it is necessary to develop another angle on the consequentiality of choice posed by Lasch. For both the ideology of consumerism and new right ideology our freedom is increased as a consequence of there being more choices available to individuals. On the face of it an increase in the number and variety of goods available on the market does suggest that consumers have more choice and, by extension, more freedom. But this fragment of simplistic thinking fails to take account of the consequentiality of choice. Most of our purchases, such as weekly food shopping, are in fact routine and thus inconsequential. In this context, the pluralisation of choice created by the proliferation of consumer goods does not signify freedom at all – it merely refers to the *pluralisation of inconsequential choice*. What kind of freedom is it that is manifested when a consumer chooses to buy one brand of chocolate biscuits in preference to another?

The pluralisation of inconsequential choice does in fact encourage a greater expenditure of time, either in deliberating over making a choice and/or in wading through all the goods that are basically the same in order to find what one wants. Given that time is a vital resource for freedom, it can be said that the so-called freedom of choice offered by the market is actually a negation of freedom. Yes, we have no choice but to choose, as Giddens argues, but that making choices has become a *requirement* ought to be reason enough not to equate freedom of choice with freedom.

The ideology of consumerism, my argument suggests, is wrong to equate consumer choice with freedom. There are further reasons why this is so, and they all, ultimately, return us to the consequences of the alienation of labour discussed earlier. These consequences essentially restrict the freedom potential of choice and autonomy. The arena of consumption limits freedom and autonomy by confining choice to 'choosing from or among', which is a far cry from the freedom implied in 'deciding or choosing for oneself'. As Bauman argues, 'Individual choices are in all circumstances confined by ... constraints.' Bearing in mind that Bauman is specifically addressing the realm of politics rather than consumption, he identifies two sets of constraints.

> One set is determined by the *agenda of choice*: the range of alternatives which are actually on offer. All choice means 'choosing among', and seldom is the set of items to be chosen from a matter for the chooser to decide.[14]

For the realm of consumption it will be more appropriate to refer simply to the *range of choice*. The second set of constraints 'is determined by the *code of choosing*: the rules that tell the individual on what ground the preferences should be given to some items rather than others and when to consider the choice as proper and when as inappropriate'.[15]

While Bauman maintains that 'Both sets of constraints co-operate in setting the frame within which individual freedom of choice operates',[16] in the hands of the ideology of consumerism the code of choosing is seen as anything but a constraint. The 'ground' for preferences is assumed to be the individual's values, which, while open to social influence, are ultimately chosen by the individual. It also assumes that an individual's values are not only indicative of what is important to the individual, which is another way of saying that an individual's values reflect his or her self-identity, but, as with self-identity, are a determinant of choice and provide direction to an individual's autonomy and freedom. Critics might consider lifestyle choices to be trivial, but for the ideology of consumerism they are important because they reflect what is important to the individual *and* they are an expression of freedom.

While it is true that an individual's values are chosen, and do indicate what is important to the individual, it cannot be assumed that choices are the materialisation of values. This assumption reflects what I referred to in the first chapter as the ideology-centredness that permeates Cultural Studies. As we have seen, it is a blinkered vision in which consumer choices are wrongly assumed to reflect symbolic values and self-identity and actually to constitute self-identity.

Bauman's code of choosing does, unintentionally, play into the hands of the ideology of consumerism. What he says about the range of choice, however, is totally ignored as a constraint. Yet, it is evident that 'choosing among' denotes far less freedom than 'deciding for oneself'. Students will know that a multiple choice (choosing among) exam or questionnaire offers far less scope for self-expression (freedom) than an exam or questionnaire that invites unsolicited and freely formulated responses. The so-called freedom of the realm of consumption is equivalent to that of a multiple choice exam or questionnaire.

Reference to 'the range of choice' invites the question: who determines the range? The obvious answer is: big business. Those involved in producing the range of goods are clearly exercising a freedom that is not available to the consumer. To deny that this is so is bizarre – it is to deny the alienation of labour.

Yet, in its more delusionary moments, the ideology of consumerism tells us that producers produce only what consumers want. The range of choices available is apparently determined by consumers – and thus whatever the problems posed by the alienation of labour, they have now been solved! We can recall Frank Mort's assertion that what is produced 'is shaped by the noises coming from the street'. Even if this is true the range of what is produced is not tailored to the preferences of *each* and *every* individual. No one consumer determines the whole range of goods. Of course, it might be the case that producers take note of what does and does not sell, survey consumer opinion on various products, and even test this opinion in relation to future products. This, however, does not add up to consumer freedom determining the range of goods. To maintain that it does is to attribute freedom to *an aggregrate* of individuals, which of course is a nonsense. Aggregates are abstractions and abstractions do not exercise freedom.

Consumer-led production is a myth and cannot be used, as the ideology of consumerism does, to advance the bigger myth of consumer freedom. As Nigel Whiteley, drawing on the testimonies of marketing and design professionals, puts it:

> 'Consumer-led' design is ... a misleading term. It implies that companies are following where consumers are leading; but its proponents admit that consumers have to be enticed to want to go to a place that they did not even know existed. A more honest term for this sort of design would be 'marketing-led', because it is marketing, not the consumer, which is the driving force.[17]

If the range of consumer choices was to reflect genuine consumer freedom, consumers themselves would have to decide what was to be produced. This is clearly not the case, and can never be the case while the power of capital remains dominant. The ideology of consumerism misleadingly wants to articulate what is a constraint on consumer choice as an example of consumer freedom.

There is, however, a most obvious constraint on consumer choice that operates within the range of goods available. The obvious constraint in question is that of money at the individual's disposal. This constraint is a *pre-condition of consumer choice*. As a constraint it simply means that the range of choices that are *practically available to the individual* are, for almost everybody, considerably fewer than the range of goods in the market place. Needless to say, any notion of freedom that is based on the ideology of consumer choice is a severely distorted one – all the more so when the concept of consumer choice fails to acknowledge all the constraints to which consumer choice is subjected.

Needs, Freedom and Affluence

The ideology of consumerism's emphasis, and celebration, of consumption as a realm of freedom does contribute to the myth of widespread affluence – a near universal affluence in the advanced capitalist societies. Of all the omissions in its theorisation of consumption, that of the crucial role of basic needs is the most serious. The absence of any notion of need from the ideology of consumerism is quite deliberate. Needs are in some way *necessitating* and thus restrictive. To understand consumption as being needs-based is to compromise it as a realm of freedom. Instead the ideology of consumerism bases its explanations of consumption on post-necessity or symbolic values, thereby promoting the image of freedom. The implication here is that consumers have moved beyond necessity (they have freed themselves from necessity) into the realm of freedom. If we no longer buy things because we need them, then presumably we do not need them – a sure sign of affluence.

Obviously almost everybody who can afford to will, from time to time, buy things that they do not need. There is no need to deny this. As I noted in Chapter 2, there is also no need to deny that symbolic or post-necessity values may play some part, though not the most important part, in our purchase of necessities. But it is sheer stupidity to discount needs-motivations as the primary source of most of what most people consume. Who, other than the most self-duped Cultural Studies academic, is going to believe that needs-motivations do not play a central role in explaining the consumption of food, water, heat, energy and so forth?

The ideology of consumerism, as I pointed out in the Introduction, justifies its discounting of needs on the basis of arguments supportive of cultural pluralism and relativism. In particular, the ideology of consumerism is satisfied that, whether or not needs exist, whether or not they are socio-culturally constructed and thus open to cultural variation, they are best thought of as relative to the individual, and thus best defined by the individual. Given the fact of individual differences, so the argument goes, it becomes impossible objectively to distinguish needs from wants. The way out of this difficulty is to replace the language of needs and wants with that of preferences. This, of course, keys in rather conveniently with the language of choice and freedom.

There is a certain logic to this kind of thinking, but it is an incomplete logic. Quite simply, we could say that our preferences reflect our needs (or wants), and thus our choices reflect our needs. In other words, preferences and choices, as we have already seen, do not necessarily reflect a freedom from necessity, but rather a little leeway in how we address needs. If we want to call this leeway 'freedom', then we are referring to a 'freedom within necessity', which clearly is not what the ideology of consumerism has in mind.

Whatever the academic difficulties posed by the concept of need, there is no legitimate justification for ignoring them. There is no justification, either, for assuming that preferences reflect individual freedom understood as a post-necessity value. But it is just this assumption that underpins the whole ideology of consumerism. And it is this assumption that takes the ideology of consumerism beyond new right ideology. Up to now, new right ideology has been in the business of creating fictions to disguise the fact that the only freedoms granted and tolerated in a capitalist world are those that do no harm to the capitalist system. These fictions, as I have stressed, are knowingly created as fictions. But these fictions, if you like, obey the rules of the realist tradition, albeit from a privileged and affluent position. At least new right ideology is sufficiently steeped in realism to know that for the vast majority consumption is about satisfying needs. In taking us beyond needs into imaginary symbolism in the name of freedom, the ideology of consumerism offers new right ideology a different kind of fiction (some would say a postmodernist fiction) for its own use.

Part Two

Explaining Individual Consumption

5 Compelled to Consume

In my critique of the latest ideology of consumerism I have drawn on a number of basic theoretical ideas that continue to have considerable experiential relevance. That many of these ideas have become unfashionable (unsexy) says more about the fickle nature of academic fashion than about the premature redundancy of potentially useful ideas. In Britain at least, recent performance imperatives in the universities may well have induced an endemic anxiety amongst academics that renders many of them more vulnerable to going along with the fashion of the day. I have attempted to communicate with the fashion victims by engaging with what has become 'trendy' in the first part of this book.

In this part of the book I shall add some detail to those ideas that strike me as most relevant for a theory of consumption. Most of my attention will be devoted to the direct and indirect consequences of employment for consumption. The alienation of labour already ensures that the satisfaction of survival needs requires a dependence on consumer goods. In other words, *we are compelled to consume.* Employment, I shall argue, reinforces this dependence by resourcing individuals, via income, for consumption, and under-resourcing individuals, by devouring time and energy, for autonomy. Obviously, in developing this argument, the triviality and irrelevance of the latest ideology of consumerism will be further exposed.

Before entirely parting company with the current orthodoxy, it will be necessary to preface my own theory of individual consumption with a few comments on how it is likely to be 'received' by advocates of the ideology of consumerism. The latter, in the growing volume of textbooks addressing consumption, is fielded as either a consumer-led approach, or an interactionist one, and definitely distinct from 'the production of consumption' approach. Consumer-led or interactionist approaches are deemed to be preferable to the production of consumption approach by virtue of accommodating certain indisputable facts. The 'facts' that are given theoretical emphasis are those that are believed to be antithetical to the production of consumption approach. These 'facts' are by now familiar: consumption involves consumers actively and creatively using goods or the images of consumer culture for symbolic purposes; consumption is meaningful and aesthetically pleasurable; consumption is the means through which we create self-identities, and so on. These 'facts' imply other facts, such as the fact that individuals are moral agents capable of exercising interpretive freedom, and that the field of consumption opens up opportunities for the expression of freedom and so on.

My critique of the latest ideology of consumerism will correctly suggest that I am operating from within a production of consumption approach. A few key words or phrases, such as 'needs', 'alienation', 'use value' (especially 'material use value'), or even 'capitalism' (rather than the more neutral and academically cleansed concepts of modernity, postmodernity, post-traditional, globalisation and so on), will have already given the game away. In today's academy, key words act as triggers instigating the automatic dismissal of whole perspectives. The production of consumption perspective is typically dismissed on the grounds that it is dated, that it arises from a redundant theoretical tradition (Marxism or neo-Marxism), that it is economistic, crude, simplistic, mechanical and elitist, and that it ignores or contradicts all those self-evident truths embodied in whatever is currently fashionable.

Only the dinosaurs of the totally irrelevant Old Left, and the baby dinosaurs of the equally irrelevant old New Left, would have the temerity or naivity to use the blunt instruments of a totally discredited perspective against the altogether more sophisticated nuances of current orthodoxy. Yet it has been a relatively simple task to demonstrate that the latest ideology of consumerism is fundamentally flawed. Likewise, I will show that the discreditation of the production of consumption perspective is also without validity. In fact, the dismissal of this perspective has been possible only because it is routinely misrepresented. Its 'simplifications' and 'crudities' – the so-called 'bluntness' of its theoretical instruments – are actually artefacts produced by its misrepresentation.

The misrepresentation of the production of consumption perspective has been largely responsible for the premature dismissal of a social theory that offers ideas that continue to be relevant for a credible explanation of consumption. At the same time this explanation enables both a radical, *non-elitist,* critique of consumer culture and a critique of the capitalist system that has spawned it. It is thus important to correct the standard misrepresentation of the production of consumption perspective.

My task in this chapter will be that of presenting the case that most, if not all, *individual consumption is best understood as obligatory rather than free*. But, given that any argument supportive of this idea, no matter how well it is empirically grounded, is automatically filtered through misrepresentations of the production of consumption perspective, it will be necessary to 'bounce' these arguments against the wall of popular misconceptions. This will be conducted in a way that discloses the essential elements of a theory of individual consumption. First, however, I shall attempt to explain how the production of consumption perspective came to be fundamentally misrepresented.

Misrepresenting the Production of Consumption

The production of consumption approach, from the viewpoint of the ideology of consumerism, it is widely alleged, mistakenly assumes that individuals have to be manipulated to become consumers – consumers are produced by producers, typically via advertising. In a simplistic, but common, misrepresentation of the production of consumption approach, Featherstone tells us that:

> The expansion of capitalist production, especially after the boost received from scientific management and 'Fordism' around the turn of the century, it is held, necessitated the construction of new markets and the 'education' of publics to become consumers through advertising and other media.[1]

Featherstone notes that 'this development is regarded as producing greater opportunities for controlled and manipulated consumption'.[2]

Bearing in mind that 'control and manipulation' is, within Cultural Studies, understood as ideological control (the control of meaning), and that ideologies or meanings are believed to govern action, any theory positing ideological manipulation via advertising and the mass media as an explanation of consumption is contradicting empirical evidence,[3] and, as Featherstone notes, 'actual processes of consumption which reveal complex differentiated audience responses and uses of goods'.[4]

The production of consumption perspective, it would seem, attempts to explain consumption as the product of the manipulative ideological power of advertising and the mass media. *Wrong.* Sure enough, some writers have pursued this path. However, the major theorists of the production of consumption perspective – Gorz and the Frankfurt School – make it absolutely clear that *consumption is not produced by advertising and the media.* Rather, they insist that *consumption is produced, in the first instance, by the alienation of labour and the subsequent organisation and experience of employment.*

Marcuse, for example, was aware that he and his Frankfurt School colleagues were misrepresented by their critics. He refers to the criticism that 'we overrate greatly the indoctrinating power of the "media" ...'. He retorts that the criticism 'misses the point. The pre-conditioning does not start with the mass production of radio and television and with the centralization of their control.'[5] Gorz elaborates:

> The passive and 'massified' consumer required by capitalist production ... is not created by capitalism altogether by means of advertising, fashion, and 'human relations', ... on the contrary, capitalism *already* creates him within the relationships of production and the work situation by cutting off the producer from his product ...[6]

Such statements are repeated across a wide range of the writings of Gorz and the Frankfurt School. Yet the production of consumption perspective continues to be misrepresented – and in ways that ensure that it is a perspective that no longer deserves attention. Symptomatic here is Jim McGuigan's reference to Mica and Orson Nava (enthusiastic supporters of the latest ideology of consumerism) whom he believes

> ... are absolutely right to reject Vance Packard's (1957) purely manipulative theory of advertising and Herbert Marcuse's (1964) philosophically sophisticated 'one-dimensional man' thesis. Both were indeed 'demeaning' to ordinary people in their time. And perhaps some intellectuals still hold a similarly pessimistic view of advertising and consumerism. But for popular cultural analysis, in the early 1990s, these are straw men from a dim and distant past.[7]

While it is true that the Frankfurt School, more so than Gorz, had plenty to say about advertising and the media, their potential influence on consumption can be understood *only* in the context of the fact that *we are forced to consume* (irrespective of the little choices we make) as a consequence of the alienation of labour and employment. This fact alone does make many of the criticisms of the production of consumption perspective redundant. It is the alienation of labour, not advertising and the media, that *ensures* that we have to purchase goods to meet our basic needs. From here the production of consumption perspective pursues a trajectory radically different from that suggested by its critics.

To argue that we are forced to consume as a consequence of the alienation of labour does not imply that individuals are duped by ideological manipulation – it is, if you like, a form of *material manipulation*. It is an acknowledgement of the powerlessness of individuals as individuals to act in ways that effectively oppose the capitalist system's control over the role of labour. By the same token it is an acknowledgement of the material power of the capitalist system to organise effectively the means through which we are to satisfy our basic needs, however these might be interpreted. Under the alienation of labour this translates into our *dependency* on employment, which alone, as we shall see later, exerts its own material manipulations on needs and consumption.

For the production of consumption perspective the power of advertising and the media to manipulate consumption pales into insignificance when compared with the material manipulations noted above. Critics have ignored this, even though it is made abundantly clear by Adorno and Horkheimer in the essay 'The Culture Industry: Enlightenment as Mass Deception'[8] that is most often singled out as theorising consumption as the product of advertising and the media. Adorno and Horkheimer stress that in comparison with 'the most powerful sectors' of the economy 'cultural monopolies are weak and dependent',[9] and operate on individuals already in the grip of more powerful forces.

Needless to say, the most powerful sectors of the economy have a direct, material impact, both on the context in which we live, which as we shall see in the next chapter is a significant factor in explaining consumption, and in determining the range of goods available. It is these sectors, too, that fund, and thus to a large extent determine, the range of cultural products produced by the culture industry.

Adorno and Horkheimer, in emphasising the material impact of the alienation of labour and employment on individuals, are in no way assuming that the subordinate are somehow to blame for their own dependence. It is 'the actual working conditions in society' which 'compel conformism ...'.[10] This is so irrespective of what individuals *think*, irrespective of how individuals interpret their dependence on the capitalist system, in short, irrespective of the ideologies which individuals might hold. As Adorno put it: 'The trouble is with the conditions that condemn mankind to impotence and apathy and would yet be changeable by human action; it is not primarily with people and with the way conditions *appear* [my emphasis] to people.'[11]

Not only this, but ideological power and its ideological effects, which, according to the critics, is what the production of consumption perspective is all about, are actually deemed to be far less important than material power and its material effects. Again Adorno makes this clear. 'Considering the possibility of total disaster, reification is an epiphenomenon, and even more so is the alienation coupled with reification, the subjective state of consciousness that corresponds to it.'[12]

(For an extension of this discussion of the misrepresentation of the production of consumption perspective, see the Digression: 'Elitism, Adorno and Football)

Survival Needs and Priorities

The manipulation of needs and consumption that occurs as a consequence of the alienation of labour and our dependence on employment, it has been emphasised, is primarily material rather than ideological, and takes place prior to the secondary, less effective and less important, ideological manipulations of advertising and the media. But talk of the material manipulation of needs, rather than restoring the credibility of the production of consumption perspective, critics might argue, merely confirms its redundancy.

Ideological manipulation is bad enough, but the manipulation of needs sounds altogether more total, perhaps biological, allowing less scope for human agency. Are not basic needs part of the discourse of instincts and drives? As such is there not a real danger of reducing human action to conditioned responses? That this manipulation is driven by material power suggests that individuals are mechanistically controlled, behind their backs so to speak. Does this not do scant justice to the complexities of human consciousness and the capacity for creative autonomy? Besides, to refer to the manipulation of needs does return us to all those notorious difficulties inherently involved in defining needs. What needs? Whose needs? What constitutes the satisfaction of a given need? Is it not the case that failure to find satisfactory answers to these questions precipitated the demise of the concept of need in social and cultural theory?

All of these questions will be addressed in what follows. However, I shall attempt to short-circuit many of the difficulties that are typically associated with the concept of need by appealing to the commonly recognised distinction between basic or survival needs, and other needs, desires or wants. This distinction, which most people make (either explicitly in sub-survival conditions or tacitly in more comfortable circumstances) is not one that is made with sufficient precision to satisfy the philosophers, but it does not have to be. It is a *general* distinction that enables most people broadly to establish priorities for courses of action. People do not act on the basis of precise conceptual distinctions, but on the basis of priorities. If we are to explain action, and in particular consumption as a form of action, then it makes good sense to tune in to people's priorities.

Priorities suggest a more immediate and precise relevance for action than, for example, general beliefs or values. An individual may claim to believe that, let us say, the world should be de-militarised, or all Third World debt should be unconditionally cancelled. Yet there is precious little that one can effectively do as an individual to materialise these beliefs. Quite simply, very few people are in a position of power with the relevant resources to act effectively on these beliefs. And those who are would have to prioritise these beliefs in order to take effective action. This implies a strong commitment on their part, that is, they must be sufficiently motivated to want to take effective action. Priorities thus embody motives to act.

According to the latest ideology of consumerism our motives to consume are of a post-necessity variety, rooted in freely chosen wants and desires – they have nothing to do with needs. The implication is that, at least in the more affluent societies, our lives are no longer dominated by the need to satisfy basic needs. We have moved on. We live in a post-scarcity society in which we are more free than ever before to attend to the 'higher' things in life.

Against this view I shall argue that our lives remain structured by the need to survive, and that for at least three-quarters of the populations of the so-called affluent societies the manipulation of this need by the social system *imposes* on them a pattern of consumption relevant to survival. In other words, most of what is consumed by most people can be best understood both in terms of its use value for addressing the need to survive and as *compulsory*. The obvious implication of my argument will be that the scope for unnecessary consumption, the speciality of the ideology of consumerism, is severely restricted for the vast majority. Furthermore, so-called unnecessary consumption – what used to be referred to as 'consumerism' – can also be best understood, not so much as compulsory, but as manipulated by the social system.

Before launching into my argument I want to make it clear that I am not about to portray consumption as little more than a simple response to basic needs. But I will argue that the need to survive, and to ensure the survival of one's dependants, does occupy a special status in the lives of *everybody* – all the more so in societies where socially provided 'guarantees' (unemployment benefits, pensions, health care and so on) for individual survival are non-existent or in decline.

The special status of survival needs derives from the fact that of all of our motives to act, only that of the need to survive (as distinct from other needs, desires and wants) *has to be regularly satisfied.* Indeed, unless they are regularly satisfied all of our wants, desires and other needs lose their motivational force. People know this well and that is why addressing survival needs takes priority from time to time. This does not mean that this is always the case, or that survival needs are foregrounded in our consciousness all of the time, or that it is even our strongest motive. But we do know that survival needs have to be addressed today, tomorrow and as far as we can see into the future, and because we know this we attempt to do what it takes to ensure our survival into the forseeable future. Thus survival needs not only order our priorities for action in the here and now, but crucially into the future.

In the more affluent societies, doing what it takes to survive from day to day is best served by future planning. And, as I shall argue, it is the priority given to 'the doing of what it takes' to satisfy survival needs that imposes a structure on our total range of activity. It is within the structure of this range of action that consumption as a form of action can be best understood.

Employment and Consumption

Under the alienation of labour, doing what it takes to survive translates, for most people, into the need for employment whether for oneself or for someone on whom one is dependent. The alternative is to be dependent on welfare benefits, which, typically, are insufficient. Being employed structures our total range of action in three fundamental ways: as the primary means to an income, as a consumer of time and as a consumer of energy. Prior to discussing the impact of these three factors on our total range of action I want to assure the reader that I am not about to embark upon explicating a mechanistic psychology.

I am recognising that the explanation of action must consider what is practically possible from the viewpoint of the individual *prior to* considerations that are more properly understood as 'psychological'. I am not disputing the fact that action involves a subject with needs, wants and desires, a subject who is a meaning-maker, who has values and beliefs, who has developed a range of capacities, has certain dispositions and inclinations and so on. Indeed, in emphasising that an explanation of action must start out from what is deemed to be practically possible from the *viewpoint of the individual subject,* I am acknowledging what individuals routinely do. Any credible psychology should take this into account.

To act implies 'being able to act', and 'being able to' cannot be understood solely in terms of the resourcefulness of the subject – his or her creativity, imagination, intelligence, prior learning, tenacity, determination and so on. Being able to act also involves possession of, or access to, resources that cannot be construed as self resources, such as public amenities, public facilities, tools, equipment and so on.

However, we can get a clear idea of the kinds of resources most people regularly consider to be important in enabling action from the reasons they often provide *for not being able to act.* 'Sorry. I can't do that. I'm working.' 'I can't do that. I can't afford it.' 'I have not got the time.' 'I'm too knackered.' Now, it could be claimed that in some instances these are not so much real reasons for not doing something, but rather excuses for not wanting to. However, the 'excuses' are rarely challenged because almost everybody knows that they could be, and often are, legitimate reasons. Everybody knows about the priority that people have to give to employment, everybody knows that time and energy are essential resources enabling action, and that money as a resource is necessary in order to do certain things. Furthermore, this knowledge is routinely drawn on by the individual in determining what action is practically possible.

Indicating common reasons for not being able to act is not only useful in identifying vital resources for action, it alerts us to the need to incorporate *the lack of resources* as an important, if not always essential, consideration in explaining action. Quite simply an explanation of why I am doing 'this' might well be found in the fact that I do not have the resources to do 'that'. This very consideration will become important for an explanation of consumption.

Employment for Survival Money

The significance of money or the lack of it for an explanation of action is self-evident. That, for most people, money comes in the form of earned income, is merely to recognise the obvious – being employed (including being self-employed), for most people, is the only 'safe' way (as distinct from the unsafe ways of illegal theft or risky gambling) of obtaining enough money to satisfy basic needs and to do other things. These 'other things', some useful, some useless, some significant, some insignificant, proliferate in proportion to disposable income. However, only a wealthy minority are in a position to spend consistently without any consideration of need. As full-time employment has become scarce, as all employment has become more insecure and as state-provided guarantees are dwindling and less secure, an increasing proportion of disposable income, for the vast majority, is being spent on future survival in the form of job loss insurance, private pensions, investments and savings, home improvements, private medical insurance and so on.

In a real sense to be employed is a priority for the vast majority for the simple reason that it provides survival money. But being employed involves the sale of labour time to an employer. This alone has a crucial effect on our range of action by virtue of reducing the time available for action outside of the hours employed. This does not mean that a greater range of action is available to the unemployed. While the availability of time is an essential resource for all action, and is especially crucial for satisfactorily addressing experienced 'existential' and identity needs, time alone is insufficient for meeting survival needs. The unemployed know this well.

In social conditions (the alienation of labour) in which most people do not have direct access to all the means necessary for their own survival, employment for a sufficient income becomes an experienced need. In other words, the alienation of labour *ensures* that most people do not possess the resources that enable them to produce for their own needs. Survival needs, for the vast majority, can be addressed *only* by the purchase of the relevant goods. This is the primary sense in which we can say that *consumption is compulsory*. Let there be no mistake about this. It is the capitalist system, through its control of labour and dictatorship over the means of survival, that makes consumption compulsory.

Consumption and Labour Time

Compulsory consumption is both reinforced and *expanded* by employers' control of labour time. The labour time lost in employment reduces the time available for producing for oneself. Obviously the more we can do for ourselves the less reliant we are on consumer products. It is in this sense that we can say that *being employed reinforces the need to consume* by consuming our time. While the level of compensation for this lost time, income, may enable us to do more than satisfy immediate survival needs, the 'doing more' is itself restricted by our loss of time and by the *inherent limitations of money*. Money buys whatever can be bought, but certain 'things' *cannot be bought* – friendship, love, solidarity, emotional security, authenticity, autonomy, creativity, intelligence, to name a few.

Of course, survival itself cannot be entirely purchased. Money buys some, but not all, of the necessary means of survival. In the interests of survival we *have to do* a number of things for ourselves and our dependants. All the activities of self-production and repro-duction, those constituting 'domestic labour' and taking care of others (what Gorz refers to as 'work-for oneself'[13] which is also work-for-ourselves) and those legally required by the system (such as paying bills and form filling) have to be conducted in time outside of employment. These activities are experienced as part of our realm of necessity in so far as they serve survival needs. But their benefits clearly exceed the need to survive. These activities are vital in the creation of a caring environment supportive of identity needs, personal autonomy and its development, and thus of human well-being and flourishing. But precisely because of the priority given to being employed, and the control of labour time by employers, *employment determines the time available for self-production and reproduction*.

Several consequences follow from this depending on the circum-stances of particular households. In high employment households, for example, in which time is scarce, a proportion (again depending on circumstances) of the tasks of self-production and reproduction may be performed, at a price, by commercial services. In other words insufficient time to do things for ourselves sets up the possibility of paying others to do these things for us. As Gorz points out this mirrors and reinforces social inequalities (our time, and thus lives, are more valuable than the time and lives of those whom we pay) and reduces the exercise, and perhaps capability, of taking care of ourselves and others.[14] In the case of important caring activities, for example child care, a substitute caring is purchased. This substitute cannot replace the caring of parents, and parents deny themselves experiences of the unconditional giving of oneself to others. Children and parents lose out. Money reigns supreme and exerts its dehumanising distortions on the socialisation of future generations.

The activities of self-production and reproduction, especially in high employment but low income households, can consume so much time that we are left with very little time that we can call 'free time'. Many women are totally familiar with this scenario and the highly restrictive effect it has on their range of action. Those who are able to afford to pay others to do their chores and more, are, in fact, buying 'free time' for themselves. However, the priority given to employment which automatically reduces our time, also ensures that 'free time' is heavily compromised.

Being employed structures our range of action by structuring our 'free time'. 'Free time' outside of employment comes in the form of brief periods of fragmented time – an hour or two here and there, the weekend and holidays. The fragmentation of free time, though worse in the case of full-time employees, and worse still in the case of those with two or more part-time jobs (even if the total hours worked are fewer than that of a full-time worker) is experienced by all employees.

Clearly the length of each stretch of free time determines what kinds of actions are possible. Certain activities can fit in neatly with brief time slots, whether these are activities that are completed in one slot or over several slots, or are ongoing. However, projects that require lengthy tracts of uninterrupted time cannot be contemplated. Needless to say, the value of fragmented free time is inherently limited. It is of little value for the development of individual autonomy, and for enabling the development of a *range* of competencies and skills that make demands of the person in terms of concentration, application, dedication and so on. In short, fragmented free time is of little value for what Gorz calls 'multi-activity'.[15]

Lengthy tracts of uninterrupted time are normally experienced during unemployment and retirement. In both cases this time is typically of limited value by virtue of the absence of other resources.

By the age of retirement most are deprived of youthful energies and are increasingly vulnerable to ill health, and some are restricted by poverty. Almost everybody has spent a life-time in which they have had to adapt to fragmented time use and are ill-prepared for doing, let alone contemplating, anything other than reproduce the kind of life imposed by employment. As Gorz observes, 'the more constricting work in its intensity and hours, the less workers are able to conceive of life as an end in itself'.[16]

Employment, Energy and Recuperation

Employment further fragments our free time by imposing on it the burden of restoring energies it (employment) has used up. In a sense before we can usefully use our already depleted and fragmented free time, we must make it usable by using it to recover sufficient energy to become active. Effortless and passive forms of recuperation become a requirement, all the more so for those employed for long hours in meaningless, mind-numbing work – the kind of work suffered by most employees today. Gorz cites the reported experience of a worker who 'tells how physical and nervous exhaustion stifles the life of a couple, erodes sexual relations ("you end up so exhausted that you completely forget the other person, you really haven't got time"), and destroys the ability to think ...'.[17]

For many, the recuperative needs that are generated by employment ensure that whatever free time there is is given over to rest and relaxation. But the very system that controls employment is not yet satisfied with its disdainful use of human beings. It attempts to colonise the free time that it has already destroyed by addressing 'our' recuperative needs that it has generated. This attempt comes in the form of the entertainment industry. It provides entertainment for our consumption, free of charge or very cheaply, which we can 'enjoy' while we are resting and relaxing, that is, when we are devoid of physical and mental energy. As Adorno and Horkheimer put it, 'the individual who is thoroughly weary must use his weariness as energy for his surrender to the collective power which wears him out'.[18]

Of course, with rare exceptions, the entertainment is of no particular merit in the sense that it can deliver escape, diversion, pleasure, fun and amusement that require no effort from the consumer. This is quite intentional. The entertainment is merely the means used for buying audiences for advertisers – it is a tool of advertising, and enables marketing to invade every home through television and radio. Junk mail is often binned unopened, but it is difficult to avoid exposure to televisual junk. People turn on their television sets for reasons other than receiving advertisements, but they receive them anyway, and at times when they are physically and mentally most vulnerable.

Advertising Re-visited

Now, from the arguments presented in this chapter it ought to be clear that we are compelled to consume irrespective of any effect advertising might have. The system's alienation of labour and employers' control of labour time and income have already done more than enough to ensure that we have to consume regardless. In fact, it is difficult to find any empirical evidence that suggests a clear link between advertising and consumption – a point I happen to share with the ideology of consumerism. I have yet to see adverts for heroin, cocaine, ecstasy, marijuana and other similar drugs. Yet the consumption of these substances has increased dramatically over the past 30 years or so. During this time there have been several advertising campaigns against their use.

This is not to say that there are no links between advertising and consumption, but we need to be careful in drawing these links. What evidence there is suggests that advertising does not influence the total volume of consumption of a type of product (cars, tobacco, washing detergent, shoes), but it *may* influence the sales of a particular brand of a product (Ford, Benson and Hedges). The emphasis is very much on the *'may influence'* – there are no guarantees. Yet companies feel compelled to advertise their particular brands. It is deemed necessary in order to announce new products or up-dated versions of old products. On top of this, advertising is viewed as essential if only to maintain the market position of a brand in relation to competing brands – failure to do so reduces its visibility. This is the real reason for advertising and why vast sums of money are poured into it even though increases in advertising are rarely reflected in sales. The US's five leading cigarette manufacturers, for example, together increased their spending on advertising in the US in 1997, compared with 1996, by almost 11 per cent, yet their sales decreased.[19]

The real, and major, effects of advertising are not to be found in their suspected manipulative influence on consumers but in their inflationary effects on the costs of products to consumers. In the case of high profile brand names the costs of advertising are incorporated in the already inflated price of the product, but these costs are minor compared to the advertising revenues recouped several times over by the consumer's display of the brand's logo. In the case of survival-relevant goods, unnecessary price inflation means that a higher proportion of household spending than ought to be necessary is spent on necessities. In low income households, in particular, this reinforces dependence on employment, and can lead to the search for additional income, either through overtime or an extra part-time job.

Unnecessary Consumption

In the next chapter I shall discuss in some detail how what was once considered unnecessary has become necessary, not because of the effects of advertising, but as a consequence of changes, over which the individual has little or no control, to our living environment. Essentially, the costs of doing what it takes to survive have, over the past 30 years, increased at a faster rate than the incomes of two-thirds to three-quarters of the workforce. This means that the scope for unnecessary consumption is much lower than we are led to believe. Based on statistics relevant to income, survival costs per average household and household spending, I shall argue that necessary consumption accounts for most of what most people consume. Only the level of income available to the wealthiest 25 per cent or so in the most affluent societies enables extravagant forms of spending to surpass the proportion of income devoted to necessary consumption. However, it is also evident that unnecessary consumption is not the sole province of the most affluent. As I noted throughout Part One there is no need to deny that post-necessity values may have some relevance in an explanation of consumption. The crucial question is: how much relevance?

In addressing this question I shall maintain that the very factors that are central to a credible explanation of necessary consumption – the impact of employment on income, time and energy – are also crucial in explaining the *capacity for unnecessary consumption*. They are crucial from the viewpoint of the individual in the two principal ways in which unnecessary consumption can be understood: as consumption that occurs after having taken care of necessity and as the penetration of post-necessity values into the taking care of necessity.

In both cases, however, post-necessity values are by definition of secondary importance in accounting for the individual's total pattern of consumption.

In saying this I am reversing the emphasis of the ideology of consumerism in which acts of consumption are assumed to reflect an individual's post-necessity values, and are then explained in psychocentric terms. My emphasis suggests that the search for meaning, pleasure and identity is not central to explaining an individual's total pattern of consumption. With a few exceptions, there is very little empirical evidence supportive of the view that post-necessity values take the form posited by the ideology of consumerism. What evidence there is, typically in the form of life-satisfaction studies, strongly suggests that post-necessity values, for a substantial majority of people, are of a non-commodifiable nature.[20] After taking care of necessity, most people it would seem prioritise what cannot be bought (or served by the images of consumer culture) – harmonious family relationships, love, friendships, solidarity with others, mutuality, autonomy and so on. Unfortunately the realisation of these values is impeded by long working hours and lack of energy.

This suggests that in addition to being mostly irrelevant for an explanation of necessary consumption, the post-necessity values on which the ideology of consumerism hinges its explanation of consumption are also mostly irrelevant for an explanation of unnecessary consumption. Our capacity for unnecessary consumption is dependent on income. For those with little energy and for whom time is scarce, unnecessary consumption takes a cheaper or a more expensive form, depending on income. Recuperative needs are essentially addressed via means of rest and relaxation and the passive consumption of cultural products. Beyond that there are little treats or more extravagant treats, cheap or expensive diversions and escapes.

Prior to reading cultural or psychological significance into unnecessary consumption, it is necessary to acknowledge that it is already manipulated before we make our 'free choices' by the impact of employment on income, time and energy. Only those with a sufficient income and with very low or no working hours potentially have the time and energy enabling a broad range of autonomous multi-activity. Obviously, the material resources available and required for autonomous multi-activity will make a considerable difference to the form that this activity takes. Additionally, of course, some individuals, through no fault of their own, may lack the psychological or self resources to benefit from low working hours.

Unnecessary consumption, because it is unnecessary, is too readily assumed by the ideology of consumerism to reflect our self-defined (autonomous) freedom. While we are certainly not compelled to participate in consumerism, I have said enough to indicate that unnecessary consumption, as an activity, is *promoted* by long working hours in conjunction with the over-provision of the one resource, money, required for consumerism. Money is of no use unless it is spent. It thus seems unremarkable that excess money should be spent, whether on time-saving gadgets, on products that enhance our autonomous activities, on savings and investments, on gifts, on pleasures or frivolities.

While long working hours and the generation of recuperative needs severely restrict our capacity for autonomous multi-activity, they are no bar to unnecessary consumption. Consumption, in contrast to autonomous activity, makes little demands on time and energy, and even less on our intellectual and creative capacities. *In many respects consumption is the opposite of autonomy and reflects a limited scope for autonomy.*

That there appear to be people who prefer to amuse themselves with the easily acquired pleasures of consumption rather than exert the sustained efforts demanded by autonomous activities, says more about the society in which individuals are socialised than about the attractions of unnecessary consumption. That socialisation appears to be heading in a direction that discourages the experience of autonomous activity and its undoubted satisfactions for future generations, speaks volumes about capitalism preparing the ground to secure its own future. If autonomy is in many respects the opposite of consumption, it is capitalism's enemy.

Consuming Culture

My arguments so far, critics may argue, are insufficient to account for the creativity, and indeed autonomy, that consumers regularly display. This failing on my part can no doubt be traced to my economic reductionism (the source of consumption is the alienation of labour, consumption depends on money, money comes from employment), my biologism (the emphasis on survival needs and energy), my unsophisticated treatment of time and my failure to consider the variety that exists within consumer culture, and how this is matched by a wide range of consumer responses.

This last failing is quite deliberate. I have wanted to avoid making speculations about the psycho-cultural reasons and motivations (meanings, aesthetic pleasures, self-identity) for the consumer preferences of individuals. These speculations could be totally irrelevant to the consumer. If these speculations are wide of the mark, or perhaps applicable only to a small minority of consumers, and then fielded as explanations for consumption, as the ideology of consumerism does, then we get false theory. When this theory is said to be founded on the lived experience of ordinary people, we get mystification. Far better to stick with what we can be sure about.

But what we can be sure of – the consequences of the alienation of labour and the impact of employment on money, time and energy – is of no interest to the Cultural Studies academic. Some would claim that the arguments that I have presented are not interesting at all, which really means that I have not attempted to engage in psycho-cultural speculation. Besides, the culture-centred critic could say that my uninteresting analysis, which does little more than crudely emphasise the significance of money, is totally irrelevant for an explanation of the consumption of cultural products. Many of these products are free or cost very little, and do tend to be actively and creatively approached by consumers – a clear case of consumption not being the opposite of autonomy.

A testing ground for highlighting the relevance or otherwise of my approach to unnecessary consumption is that of the consumption of television entertainment. It is available to almost everybody, it is very cheap and is widely considered by media professionals and Cultural Studies academics to offer sufficient variety to appeal to a wide range of tastes and pleasures, and provide the symbolic resources with which audiences can actively and creatively construct meaning, including self-identities. Encouraged by the consistently high viewing figures for particular programmes, the tabloid press thinks nothing of devoting several pages to matters centred on television entertainment. The assumption here is that television entertainment is important to people, and that a good way to sell adult comics (tabloid newspapers) is to provide ample coverage of what is popularly deemed to be important.

Cultural Studies academics go along with this assessment of what is important to ordinary people. In their eager elaboration of 'the interesting' they focus on the unremarkable fact that audiences are capable of a wide range of interpretive responses and symbolic uses of popular television entertainment. Not surprisingly by the late

1980s a picture of a critical, playful, creative and active audience had become an incontestable truth. People's interaction with television entertainment is thus regarded as indisputably pleasurable and meaningful. And because it is so regarded it is automatically assumed to be significant to viewers. Cultural Studies academics already knew, from viewing figures, that television entertainment was significant, but now they could identify the reasons for its significance. These reasons are, of course, all the psycho-cultural babble that Cultural Studies academics find so interesting.

The little empirical research (ethnographic studies) that has been conducted on audience interpretations of television entertainment has tended to focus on interpretations of particular programmes, and allows the audiences that are researched no scope for suggesting that they don't take the entertainment seriously enough to engage inter-pretatively with it. At least such responses are not reported. It is as if the researched audience is trapped by the researcher's assumption that it is a fact that audiences interpret. The researcher is thus only concerned with the question: 'What is your interpretation?' It would take a brave research subject, especially if he or she was being paid much needed cash to participate in the research, to respond with: 'I don't give a fuck.' So, the research subject plays the game by making an appropriate response. This is treated on an equal footing with all the reported interpretations regardless of their significance or otherwise to those (the research subjects) offering them.

The essential problem with audience research that is framed by and supportive of the ideology of consumerism is that in its rush to excavate the play of meaning (and the play of identity) in viewing television, and the pleasures experienced from viewing, it fails to ask the audience a fundamental question: 'How significant to you, in the total order of things, are the meanings and pleasures you claim to derive from television entertainment?' Where this question has been asked it is evident that whatever meanings people derive from viewing television, they are typically not considered to be meaningful, and likewise the pleasures of viewing compare poorly with other sources of pleasure.[21] In other words, Cultural Studies academics have attributed significance to what audiences consider to be insignificant. What audiences consider to be insignificant cannot be used to explain the appeal of television entertainment.

Not only is all the psycho-cultural babble about audiences wrong, it is demeaning to 'the ordinary person' in so far as the variable drivel element of television entertainment, which almost everybody can recognise, is attributed with a significance for audiences that it clearly does not possess. When the significance of drivel is then articulated in terms of the identity value of television entertainment, cultural theory is painting a picture of the audience as 'pathetic'. This surely invites the criticism that cultural theory of this type is elitist – an elitism in the name of populism.

So, prior to embellishing an explanation of unnecessary consumption in psycho-cultural terms, it is advisable to establish the significance or otherwise of unnecessary consumption in people's lives. With regard to television entertainment, any credible explanation of its 'appeal' must take into account its limited value as a source of pleasure and meaning. Why do certain groups of people spend so much time doing something (watching television) that they would rather give up in favour of more meaningful and pleasurable activities?

The answer to this question begins to reveal itself in noting those groups – the housebound (including children of pre-school age), the infirm, the unemployed, the retired – that are consistently reported as watching television in excess of 25 hours per week. It is within these groups that we find society's poorest people. One obvious source of television's appeal is its cheapness. This might not be of interest to the Cultural Studies academic, but it is, all the same, an important consideration. Of course, it cannot be the only consideration.

As we have already seen, employment may provide an income that enables individuals to participate in a wide range of activities. But this range can be severely restricted by the fragmentation of time and experienced recuperative needs. Television programme schedules are sensitive to the fragmentation of time, and are planned in ways that are compatible with the temporal structure of the lives of its targeted audience(s). Bits and pieces of time that are of little value for doing all sorts of things, can nevertheless be used for some activities, like television viewing. Some would say that the controllers of television entertainment are equally sensitive to recuperative needs in so far as what is offered can be effortlessly received and enjoyed. Recuperative needs do arise out of weariness. Their satisfaction is most likely to be sought in ways that do not further deplete the individual of energy that is not available. Television entertainment fits the bill.

This is not to say that all viewing is recuperative (effortlessly passive), or that there might be programmes that people want to watch, and that some meaning and pleasure can be derived from viewing. But it is premature speculation, and mistaken, to theorise recuperative viewing as 'active' and 'creative'. Besides, compared with the activity and creativity normally associated with autonomous activities, consumption of television entertainment, or the consumption of anything else for that matter, is passive.

The vast majority of people are not resourced, in terms of money, time and energy, all taken together, for an active, gratifying and satisfying engagement in a broad range of autonomous activities. The sphere of autonomous activities is thus restricted, and people have to opt for less meaningful and satisfying activities. In this brief discussion it is clear that the consequences of employment for income, time and our energy levels do have an important part to play in explaining unnecessary consumption and the forms that it is likely to take for different groups of people. Above all, however, the scope for expensive forms of unnecessary consumption is far more limited than the images of 'the affluent society' suggest. I will pursue this theme, in an entirely different way, in the following chapter.

6   Compelled to Consume More

Increases in the total volume of consumer spending over the past 30 years in the advanced capitalist societies, brief recessionary periods apart, are widely assumed to indicate a growing affluence. This view is often tempered by an acknowledgement that at any one time up to one-quarter of the populations of these societies live in poverty. In other words, the growth in consumer spending is largely attributable to the growing affluence of the remaining three-quarters. The implication is that the better-off are able to spend more, and since, by definition, they do not suffer need-deprivation, their extra spending goes on post-necessity goods, services and experiences. This is confirmed by common observations that car ownership and the ownership of all the 'mod cons', for example (except among the very poor) has almost reached saturation point. Then, of course, it is pointed out that almost everybody can afford foreign holidays, and that the affluent three-quarters of the population are increasingly taking more than one holiday per year.

If we want proof that the vast majority are more affluent than they have ever been we need look no further than official statistics on individual earned income. Comparisons of median earned income over the past 30 years or so reveal a steady upward trend. Additionally, it can be noted that while unemployment has encroached, at times, into the lives of the better-off, the total number of people employed today has never been as high. This is often taken to mean that median household incomes have increased at a faster rate than individual incomes.

It would seem that those who insist that the vast majority are better off have a valid argument. However, things are far more complicated than income statistics suggest. Gorz and Claus Offe maintain that since the mid-1970s the purchasing power of the majority of the populations of the advanced capitalist societies is decreasing.[1] Temporary loss of earnings due to redundancy and periods of unemployment and under-employment alone have had a depressing effect on purchasing power. Neither has the purchasing power of households increased as a consequence of more people being employed. Almost all the growth in the total number of people employed since the late 1980s has come in the form of part-time employment.[2] The vast majority of the 'new' employees are women on low pay and without the full quota of employment rights.

My particular concern in this chapter is not so much to provide conclusive evidence and arguments that the purchasing power of the majority is decreasing, but rather to support the more specific contention that the *scope for unnecessary consumption is, for approximately three-quarters of the populations of the affluent societies, decreasing.* While purchasing power is a precondition of unnecessary consumption, the latter, unlike the former, implies a distinction between necessary and unnecessary consumption.

I have already acknowledged that this is a difficult distinction to make, and that it cannot be made with any precision. However, in much the same way as most people do distinguish between survival needs and other needs, wants and desires, most people do make rough and ready distinctions between necessary and unnecessary purchases. As we shall see the underlying reason for our reduced scope for unnecessary consumption is that over the past 30 years *survival costs have increased at a faster rate than increases in incomes.*

Thus, far from reflecting post-necessity growth, increases in consumer spending, apart from the spending of a very wealthy minority, mostly reflect an increase in survival costs. This is due to price inflation of a few basic necessities, especially housing, and to an expansion of the role of *individual consumption* in the realm of necessary consumption. Crucial in theorising the latter will be those observations of Offe and Gorz that alert us to ways in which capitalist societies induce and impose 'new' means of addressing survival needs. How this has come about will be discussed in detail throughout this chapter. Before then it will be necessary briefly to address my estimation that the scope for unnecessary consumption, for approximately three-quarters of the population, is far more restricted than the images of 'the affluent society' suggest.

The Affluent Society?

Will Hutton refers to the 'thirty, thirty, forty society', respectively the percentages of the British population whom he calculates are the 'disadvantaged', the 'marginalised and the insecure', and the 'privileged'.[3] While he is referring to Britain, the powerful practices that have created these divisions do operate throughout the advanced capitalist societies. Hutton bases his divisions on a detailed analysis of employment status – unemployed, part-time, temporary, fixed-term contract, full-time and so on – and thus on income and employees' rights.

The scope for post-necessity spending is obviously severely restricted for the 'disadvantaged' – the unemployed or economically inactive, and the unofficially unemployed (those who do not figure in official statistics). Greater, but variable, purchasing power is available to the middle group – the marginalised and the insecure. But, as Hutton argues, this 'category is not so much defined by income as by its relation to the labour market'.[4] These are the intermittently employed in temporary, part-time, fixed-term or generally insecure employment. The very fact that the employment is insecure seriously restricts post-necessity spending. As I noted in the previous chapter, the knowledge that current employment may be temporary obliges employees to use a proportion of their income to address future survival.

Intermittent employment is a product of the direction pursued by all major capitalist enterprises. It is not a temporary blip. More recent employment statistics than those available to Hutton indicate that the intermittently employed now constitute more than half of the work force. I would thus revise downwards Hutton's designation of 40 per cent of the population as 'privileged'. However, as Hutton admits, the 'privileged' group, which is made up of full-time, fairly secure employees and the permanently self-employed, is split between rich and poor. He points out that 'thirty-five per cent of full-time employees ... earn less than 80 per cent of the median wage'.[5] This means that the scope for unnecessary consumption that is consistent with images of affluence is available to only 65 per cent of the 'privileged' group, or 26 per cent of the population, according to Hutton's calculations.

My own calculations suggest that the 'privileged' group is already reduced to 20 per cent of the population by virtue of the increase in intermittent employment. However, this has disproportionately reduced the number of low income, full-time employees, and thus does not suggest a further reduction of this category. Nevertheless, it can be seen that my estimation that 75 per cent of the population has far less scope for unnecessary consumption than we are led to believe is, if anything, a little conservative.

While it can be argued that among the intermittently employed there are some very high earners, whatever distortion this creates for my own estimations would have to be offset against the growth of single person households. Individual survival costs in households of two or more people are less than in single person households (two people can live more cheaply than one). These have doubled in Britain over the past 30 years and now constitute 30 per cent of all households.[6] More people are thus assuming sole financial responsibility for maintaining households. Most single person households are made up of middle-aged and older people whose purchasing power has been reduced by loss of a partner through divorce or death and/or by retirement. More recently, young professionals (mainly women) are choosing to live alone for benefits that are deemed to be preferable to an increased scope for unnecessary consumption.

That the purchasing power and scope for unnecessary consumption has been declining for a vast majority is consistent with statistics relevant to the distribution of wealth. An increasing proportion of the incomes of the wealthiest 25 per cent is unearned, and it is the investments of the very wealthiest of this group that provide an income that enables routine forms of extravagant spending. In Britain 25 per cent of the population owns 75 per cent of the wealth.[7] In the US, as Gorz points out, 'two-thirds of American economic growth went into the pockets of 1 per cent of the working population'[8] in the 1980s.

The beneficiaries of economic growth are the shareholders and chief executive officers of major companies. Gorz notes that in the 1980s

the pre-tax profits of the 500 largest American companies rose on average by 92 per cent. In 1987, 61 per cent of those profits (as against 22 per cent in 1953) went to the chief executive officers (CEOs) of those firms and in many cases the dividends paid to shareholders increased fourfold.[9]

John Kenneth Galbraith produces a similar story.

In 1980, the chief executive officers of the three hundred largest American companies had incomes twenty-nine times that of the average manufacturing worker. Ten years later the incomes of the top executives were ninety-three times greater. The income of the average employed American declined slightly in those years.[10]

These trends have continued throughout the economies of all the advanced capitalist societies. In 1992 the top executives of the 500 largest American companies earned on average 145 times as much as all blue- and white-collar workers, and by 1994, 187 times as much.[11]

William Greider writes:

> ... American workers who had lost their jobs in the recessionary years of 1990–92 suffered a 23 percent drop in wages, on average, when they found full-time work again. The news that corporate profits reached a twenty-five year high in 1994 and the stock market regularly achieved new price peaks was not especially comforting to most wage earners. Among male workers, 80 percent saw their wages stagnate or decline. For the median wage earner, pay had shrunk in real terms, by one percent a year, every year from 1989 through 1994.[12]

It is evident that the images of affluence that we are constantly supplied with are contradicted by the harsher realities experienced by at least three-quarters of the populations of the advanced capitalist societies. Yet all of these societies continue to register more or less continuous economic growth and with it an increase in the wealth produced. That this wealth is created by a mix of betting on financial markets and the stock exchange,[13] the ruthless exploitation of labour,[14] the theft of natural resources and, as we shall see, the deliberate 'ripping-off' of consumers, is of little concern to the wealthy and their apologists, and to those small-minded academics responsible for peddling the cosy ideology of consumerism.

That most people in the advanced capitalist societies are able to afford little treats, sometimes by compromising the satisfaction of survival needs, is, it would seem, reason enough to be silent on the growing inequalities in wealth, incomes and purchasing power. It is, it would seem, reason enough to be silent on the blatant lie that everybody benefits from the risk-taking and ingenuity of major investors, chief executives and senior managers. It is, it would seem, reason enough silently to condone the obscene rewards that these geniuses pay themselves. It is, it would seem, reason enough to pretend to be blind to what is emerging before our eyes: a world in which finance capital and major companies have carved out an enclave of affluence for a minority, and in which the majority are mere fodder to be abused (as disposable labour with no alternative but to buy basic necessities) by the minority. It is evident that both new right ideology and the latest ideology of consumerism are mistaking crumbs of comfort for a life of pleasure and meaning.

For the remainder of this chapter I shall discuss various ways in which an increasing proportion of the reduced purchasing power of the majority is devoted not to consumerism (unnecessary consumption) but to consumption relevant to survival. Needless to say what follows is intended to demonstrate further the irrelevance of the latest ideology of consumerism in the lives of 'ordinary people'. Where this ideology attributes the increasing levels of consumption to the free choices enabled by our growing affluence, I shall argue the opposite. Quite simply I shall demonstrate that most of what we consume, especially our most significant purchases, are not post-necessity choices, but rather choices that are externally induced. By this I mean that our choices in consumption increasingly reflect *socially induced (rather than autonomous) means of addressing survival needs.*[15]

Increasing Survival Costs

As I noted earlier the costs incurred in addressing survival needs have, over the past 30 years, increased at a faster rate than incomes. My purpose here will be to explain how this has come about. The increase in survival costs is attributable, either directly or indirectly, to the profit motive. The latter manifests itself in a number of inter-related factors that are essentially of four types: 'new' sources of profit; the exploitation of the transfer of the responsibility for need provision from the state to the individual; the exploitation of changes to the social and physical living environment, and, closely interwoven with these three factors, changing labour requirements.

New Sources of Profit

As we shall see later, the decline of state-provided services and facilities has opened up opportunities for profit in a wide range of areas such as health, education, transport, recreation, communication, energy and so on. Those so inclined have also found ample scope for profit in all the 'developments' that have effectively transformed our living environment. The re-location of work alone, for example, has opened up housing to marketisation and new developments that are ripe for profiteering. My immediate concern, however, is with those sources of profit which, while by no means new, have taken on new forms or have encroached into new areas. I shall focus on three such sources of profit: the integration of the superfluous within basic necessities, planned obsolescence and the expansion of commodification. These sources of profit have played a significant role in increasing the costs of survival by increasing the price of basic necessities.

Products may serve a number of functions, but increasingly basic products incorporate non-functional features that are *superfluous* to their utility. The superfluous is open to constant revision and thus 'newness' or novelty. Indeed, as I have noted on a number of occasions, the integration of the superfluous within basic necessities has made it impossible to refer to 'basic necessities' with any precision. Yet it is only by assessing the use value of a product for the sufficient satisfaction of survival needs that we are able to identify the superfluous. Failure to do this can, as is the case with the ideology of consumerism, lead to ignoring the continuing relevance of use value, and to misconstruing consumption altogether.

The superfluous can take a variety of forms, from unnecessary gadgetry to packaging. Its primary function is that of increasing the cost of the product. As Gorz notes, 'the usefulness of an object becomes the *pretext* for selling superfluous things that are built into the product and multiply its price'.[16] The 'pretext' is, of course, what enchants and totally absorbs the ideology of consumerism. Finn Bowring elaborates:

> The superfluous and the necessary have become inextricable components of today's commodities, and nowhere is this more apparent than in the billions of hours wasted in promoting goods which are, *in their essence,* quite necessary (food, drink, clothes, washing powder, even cars).
>
> There is no doubt that people need these products. What people do not need is the sophisticated processes by which nominally identical products are superficially embellished, symbolically differentiated and regularly upgraded, with reciprocally escalating costs, in order to lure customers away from possible competitors.[17]

Bowring comments that 'what is most objectionable about the wasteful character of modern consumerism is not the falsity of the needs that are satisfied so much as the profligate manner in which real needs are met.'[18]

The incorporation of the superfluous into basic necessities does, by increasing the chances of a product's failure, contribute to the *planned obsolescence* of the product. Planned obsolescence refers to the various ways in which producers produce goods that are less durable than they could be. Clearly it is in the interests of producers to produce goods that reliably serve the functions for which they are purchased. But it is not in the interests of producers to make things that are so durable and reliable that they will never need to be replaced. Thus a product's limited life is purposefully planned in order to ensure frequent purchases. No product is exempt from planned obsolescence. Reported annual increases in consumer spending is in part attributable not to increasing affluence, not to an insatiable desire to consume, but because the fridge, or the washing machine, or the toilet seat, for example, have a planned, unnecessarily restricted life. Major manufacturers of more expensive products, such as cars and household electrical appliances do provide replacement parts, a repair service and expensive insurance schemes to 'protect' the consumer against the possibility of exhorbitant repair and replacement costs. These are merely a means of cashing in on planned obsolescence. Often a monopoly is exercised in these services by approved dealers by dint of the fact that many repairs require the replacement of 'sealed units' that are available only through the approved dealer.

A growing practice, and one entirely consistent with the logic of planned obsolescence, is to produce goods that cannot be repaired, or where the high cost of repair acts as an inducement to replace the product. Many necessary consumer durables have become consumer disposables. In recent times this has taken on a new dimension – manufacturers nowadays are, through advertising, attempting to make a virtue out of disposability by linking it with fashion, and by promoting the 'latest fashion' as 'the ultimate'. Gorz refers to this as 'accelerated obsolescence'.

> Competitiveness demanded maximum mobility, fluidity and rapidity in designing new products and putting them into production. Firms had to be capable of continual improvisation; they had to know how to whip up passing fads, unpredictable and transient fashions, and exploit them to the full. In virtually saturated markets, the only type of growth possible was growth in the variety of taste and fashion, growth in the speed at which these things changed.[19]

As I noted in Chapter 3 this does not mean that consumers are driven by a desire to be fashionable (although a few are). More important is the fact that 'the fashionable' is actually built into products that people need, and they often have no alternative but to buy the latest fashionable product because nothing else is available. The very imperatives of competition that have stimulated accelerated obsolescence ensure the premature take-over or disappearance of companies that fail to compete. This often results in the disappearance, and thus obsolescence, of their products, replacement parts and repair services, and thus generates the need to buy a new product.

Novel ways of making profits in saturated markets can only lead to escalating the costs of survival. The poor know this well. They are accustomed to maintaining a clear distance from retail outlets selling new products, and instead attempt to satisfy their survival needs by purchasing used, obsolete products that have been 're-conditioned' in ways to ensure a temporary after-life. Entrepreneurs, without the capital to match the obscenities of major manufacturers, impose their own brand of skulduggery on the poor.

Entrepreneurship in all of its styles has, over the past 30 years or so, found lucrative opportunities beyond the over-populated saturated markets. Markets have expanded where once they were small, as for example in housing, or have been created where once they did not exist. What was at one time considered to be more of a right than a commodity, for example, health, pensions and education, has, in recent times become *commodified* and thus open to profitable exploitation and with it an unparalleled escalation in survival costs. Marketisation, and thus commodification, it would seem, know no boundaries and are part and parcel of the increasing commercialisation of everyday life.

While some of these developments have been most spectacular in areas that have no relevance to survival needs, for example the growth of merchandising associated with football clubs, what concerns me here is their impact on survival costs. The extent of this impact can be best understood in the context of the transfer of survival costs from the state to the individual, a changing social and physical environment, and a changing labour market.

Privatising Survival

The early post-war period was one in which almost all of the advanced capitalist societies (the US apart) developed welfare systems that more or less provided all sorts of survival-relevant guarantees. At least from the 1980s onward, however, these guarantees – free health care, sufficient pension provision, subsidised housing, free schooling, subsidised services and utilities, unemployment benefit and so on – have been progressively withdrawn. Capitalist states do vary in their commitment to social welfare, but the trend is very much toward reduced social provision.[20]

Whatever the reasons for this trend, only the rich have been able to protect themselves from the more significant consequences, usually by paying themselves salaries that enable them to purchase services without any effect on their standard of living. As for the majority, they have had to devote an increasing proportion of their incomes to survival costs. Indeed, governments are openly recognising that as the proportion of retired people in the total population increases, state-provided pensions may have to be reduced in value and/or restricted to the most needy.

In many of the advanced capitalist societies the state-provided pension is already insufficient to meet survival costs. For some this basic pension is supplemented by (or is a supplement to) employment-based pension schemes in which a proportion of employees' incomes are paid into a pension fund. (The so-called employer's 'contribution' to such schemes is a misnomer – the contribution is, in fact, unpaid labour stolen by the employer and then generously given back to the employee.) But with a majority of the working population in intermittent employment, employment-based pension schemes cannot provide many with the security required. Hence, the growing market in private pension schemes. This market, however, while driven by the need to secure future survival, is limited to those who can afford to make worthwhile regular payments. In other words private pension schemes run up against the same difficulties as employment-based schemes. These problems are widely recognised and prompt those who can afford it to put aside occasional and irregular savings which invariably compare unfavourably with pension plans.

Saving for the future, through a pension scheme or otherwise, has become an individual requirement. This is not to say that we all automatically do what is required of us. Many young people, understandably, put considerations of future survival on hold. After all, for the majority (two-thirds of the population do not earn enough to pay into a private pension plan likely to yield a sufficient pension),[21] taking care of the future invariably means compromising the satisfaction of immediate survival needs. During a period when governments are urging individuals to address their future survival on a privatised basis, policies have been enacted that make this impossible for all but a minority. The most significant of these policies concerns housing.

State spending on housing in Britain, as a percentage of GDP, fell from 4.2 per cent in 1975 to 2.1 per cent in 1995[22] and has continued to fall. During more or less the same period, home ownership has increased from just over half of the housing stock to over 70 per cent. Insecure private tenancies, often with inflated rents, combined with a massive decline in the availability of low rent public housing, have steered people toward home ownership – there is no alternative for the vast majority. The latter typically involves mortgage repayments. Initial mortgage repayments as a proportion of average incomes have increased from 25 per cent in the 1960s to between 30 and 45 per cent today.[23] Rented public accommodation, in Britain at least, has become restricted to those on the lowest incomes. But even now in what have become ghettoes the proportion of income spent on rent has risen to approximately 30 per cent compared with 6.4 per cent in 1979/1980.[24]

It is clear that the decline in state-subsidised housing has had a significant impact on increasing survival costs incurred by individuals. While the transfer of survival costs from the state to the individual has been most marked in the case of housing, this transfer can also be noted in health care, education, transport and utilities. The privatisation and de-regulation of public transport and utilities (electricity, gas, water) has resulted in costlier (and inferior) services. Rail travel, in Britain at least, is so expensive that it is regularly affordable only by the more affluent – it no longer constitutes a form of public transport: that is transport for the public.

Inadequate and expensive public transport is the main reason why car ownership is moving toward saturation point. Many individuals, particularly those in suburban and rural locations, find that public transport that enables them to travel to and from their place of employment, shops and amenities, can be used only at a financial cost that they cannot afford and a time cost that severely eats into 'their' time. In these circumstances people are more or less obliged to purchase their own means of private transport.

The decrease in and withdrawal of survival-relevant state-provided services for families and individuals does mean that, for the vast majority, addressing survival needs has, over the past 30 years, taken up an increasing proportion of income. Crucially, state provision for the public (as distinct from big business) has decreased during a period of accelerating social and environmental change, which has generated the need for more expensive means of addressing survival needs.

Survival in a Changing Environment

The environment in which contemporary life is conducted is quite different from that of a mere 30 or 40 years ago. Even then significant changes were afoot. Gone were the days when most people lived all of their lives in one locality, when the physical and social context of daily life had a stable continuity. These were the days when almost everybody would go to school, get a job, get married, raise a family, shop, socialise, play and die in the same locality into which they were born. Generations of the same family lived in close proximity to each other, and this enabled families to take care of 'their own' – the children, the elderly, the sick and the disabled. Beyond this it was possible to develop and maintain enduring social ties and co-operative activities with neighbours and others nearby.

These kinds of observations are often used to preface a romanticised discourse on the golden age of community life. Thus we are told that in 'the old days' children played safely in streets that were not colonised by cars, neighbours regularly interacted with each other and could be called upon for help when required, mothers met daily in the local shop, people got together to produce their own community entertainment (very few people had television), to run their own football team, to arrange outings for children and the elderly, and so on. Whatever the relative validity of these observations, and their failure to acknowledge the oppressive and repressive features of community life, such as the lack of privacy, or the imposition of pressures to conform to a restrictive morality, they nevertheless are useful in illustrating the differences between 'then' and 'now'. More than this, much of what we now consider to be necessary purchases did not figure in household budgets. Indeed, some of these items, mobile phone costs for example, could not figure because mobile phones did not exist.

When, and where, it was possible to get to work on foot, by bicycle, or by a short bus journey, there was *no need* for a car and all the costs that go with it – tax, insurance, MOT, maintenance, repair, petrol. When, and where, people in need of help could get it by alerting a neighbour there was *no need* for quick, direct access to a telephone. When, and where, families and neighbours took care of pre-school children there was *no need* to buy the services of a child-minder. All of these examples, and more, such as the need for residential homes for the frail and the elderly, the need for private transport to access retail parks, the need for state-subsidised or commercially-provided services to feed or administer continuous 'health care' to the infirm, suggest that much of what counts as necessary expenditure today was, in earlier times, either not necessary or was available free of charge.

But these examples also indicate that the social and environmental context in which we live does have a significant influence on how we address survival needs and on what can be regarded as basic necessities. There is little doubt, too, that changes to our social and physical environment have actually *imposed* on individuals costlier means of addressing survival needs. In saying this, I am not implying that all change is bad. I am merely stating a fact about survival costs. And when I refer to 'costlier means of addressing survival needs' I am not alluding to individuals *choosing* extravagant ways of addressing needs. I am referring to the extra costs that are *necessarily* incurred as a consequence of survival in today's environment that *from the standpoint of the individual make practical and economic sense.*

The possession of a car, for example, from the viewpoint of most of those who own one, is not a luxury. That modern cars embody luxury (superfluous) features is not the point. The costs of private car ownership and travel, in spite of their emergence as the second highest item of expenditure for a majority of household budgets, are, for many, lower than the costs of making necessary journeys on 'public' transport. Thus from the viewpoint of the individual, ownership of a car is economically rational. It is, if you like, the private solution to travel needs that have emerged in an environment in which what is publically provided is inadequate and too expensive.

In many respects some of the most noticeable changes to our physical environment – a more intricate network of motorways, roads and streets, increasing areas of space devoted to car parks, out of town retail outlets – are the result of policies intended to accommodate private car use. And as our urban and rural landscape is re-fashioned to suit private motoring the latter becomes ever more rational from the viewpoint of the individual. Of course, what makes sense from the viewpoint of the individual can produce consequences that are socially and environmentally irrational. The increasing volume of traffic alone produces time-costly and fuel-costly bottlenecks, heightens the possibility of accidents with their attendant costs to both the individual and emergency services, and pushes up the health costs of pollution.

It is not my intention to present a wholly negative slant on what might be regarded as 'progress'. I am merely concerned to point out that changes in our social and physical environment, in conjunction with factors already discussed, generate survival costs that have to be borne by the individual. Some of these additional survival costs do benefit the individual, as in the case of improved housing, and some, quite frankly, do not, as in the case of having to pay more for water that is undrinkable. But, as we have seen in the case of cars, things are rarely this simple. The positives and negatives of social change are intertwined, as are the positives and negatives of the survival strategies that we adopt in response to these changes. On top of this, positives that are intended to solve or remove negatives, may actually create an entirely different set of negatives and with them a different set of new costs to the individual. This can be illustrated with respect to housing.

Most will agree that for most people their immediate living environment (the house or flat) is of a higher quality than was the case just 30 years ago. This improved quality – better insulation, more efficient heating, better lighting, the elimination of dampness and its attendant health risks – is a positive. On the negative side, it can be noted that these improvements have come at the expense of a greater risk of accidents and personal injury, increasing toxicity, poorer air quality and new health hazards. For example, it is frequently noted that a growing proportion of injuries in the home are due to the misue of electrical equipment, including power tools, and that the use of many electrical goods increases exposure to electromagnetic fields and thus heightens the risk of cancer.[25] A further negative is that of extra financial costs. A better insulated and heated house, for example, not only costs more, but generates the need for a refrigerator in which to store perishable foods.

The particular point that I want to make here is that many of the changes that are often associated with progress eliminate one set of problems only to produce a new set. Invariably the new problems, as in the case of health, overburden state-provided services. Thus, in Britain for example, in spite of increased spending on the health service, a growing number of people are having to seek and pay for alternative or private forms of treatment. While for a majority these new costs may not add up to much, for the chronically ill (who typically are disqualified from private health insurance schemes) these costs may be considerable.

No doubt many of the new illnesses and viruses are due to new environmental conditions, in the home, in the processed and preserved food that we eat, in the use of pesticides and in the differently polluted wider environment. There is no doubt, either, that there are environmental factors contributing to the increase in incidence of immune-system disorders, hormone-based illnesses, asthma, allergies and cancers, for example. And no doubt individuals will have to pay for an increasing proportion of the costs of treating and managing environmentally-induced health problems.

These remarks are not intended to 'rubbish' the health professions, or those governments that do increase their spending on health care. Great strides have been made to eliminate and manage those health problems about which we have sufficient knowledge to produce successful treatments. But the problem with new health risks is that as yet there is insufficient research and knowledge about them. Given that over half a million chemicals are regularly used in modern life, and the number is increasing, and given that we are, amongst other things, bio-chemical beings, it would be most surprising if new health problems did not arise. As Sandy Irvine and Alec Ponton point out, 'we know next to nothing about their [the chemicals] interaction and combined effects, and the scale of the problem suggests that we never will'.[26]

I acknowledge that a proportion of health costs to the individual and the state are unnecessary in so far as they arise from avoidable accidents or unhealthy lifestyle choices, such as excessive use of alcohol and tobacco, nutritionless food, or even sexual activity. Environmentally-induced health problems, however, are propelled by an economic system over which the individual has no control. Faced with debilitating symptoms, about which the medical profession is mostly clueless, individuals, understandably, try to sort things out for themselves, and at a cost. It is no accident that the 'health market' has recently expanded. Numerous therapies offering 'helpful' treatments and cures and health shops selling often bogus remedies await the custom of the desperate and vulnerable.

Changes in our social and physical environment, as we have seen, increase the proportion of income that must be devoted to survival costs. Of course, this is not to say that all change produces this particular consequence. However, it is no accident that survival costs have increased in proportion to increases in income. I am not implying a conspiracy here. But we have seen a number of ways in which the capitalist system has elaborated and extended the common observation that what you are given (increased wages) with one hand, the system takes back (increased prices) with the other.

Cashing in on the priority that people give to survival needs has always been one of the principal ways in which the capitalist system controls people's lives. In more recent times this type of control has taken on new dimensions as capitalism itself changes. Capitalism's power is increasingly concentrated in fewer transnational companies which, in conjunction with finance capital (banks, insurance companies, pension funds), exercise a stranglehold on the global economy. Not so long ago major enterprises were content (or seemed to be) to realise, by today's standards, a modest, steady rate of profit. Many bosses believed that their profit-making ambitions could be achieved over the long term by a level of investment sufficient to maintain continuous production. All of this has changed.

Production processes have been revolutionised by the use of micro-electronic technologies. As a consequence major companies are able to increase their profits at the same time as reducing their labour costs and investments. And huge annual (and preferably, quarterly) increases in profits are deemed to be the best way of attracting the major investors away from other, less profitable, companies. In this context, in which massive amounts of finance capital can be switched, almost at a moment's notice, from one company to another, the pressure to produce ever-higher profits eventually, and inevitably, leaves its mark on employment and the costs of consumption. In short, the pace and volume of 'market transactions' creates a highly unstable labour market.

Being employed is the principal means of obtaining income. But when the labour requirements of capitalism are subjected to accel-erating modification, as they are now, we must, in the interests of our own survival, try our hardest to remain in employment while keeping an eye out for other employment just in case we lose our current jobs. More than this, to achieve any kind of continuity of being employed, we must be prepared to move. When in any one year between 5 and 10 per cent of the population move home, any kind of stability to our local social environment is difficult to achieve. We have already noted some of the knock-on survival costs of being physically uprooted from family, friends and neighbours. To this we must add the costs of moving itself.

Changing Labour Requirements

One important consequence of the alienation of labour is that employment opportunities broadly determine where and how we live. Throughout the last century, and a bit before, the industrialisation of agriculture produced a steady flow of redundant farm workers into the cities and towns in search of employment. And, later on in the century, millions of workers found themselves out of work as heavy industry and manufacturing re-located in the Third World. These workers chased new employment opportunities in their locality, but inevitably, for many, employment could be found only far afield.

Whereas in the recent past most individuals would move home two or three times during their lifetime, today we can expect to move far more often. Compared to today, in the 1950s through to the mid-1970s, more people moved home as a consequence of urban renewal programmes – 'slum clearance', new housing developments, new towns and so on. Today, however, the main reason for frequent moves is that of changing jobs, not out of choice, but because of accelerating fluctuations in the labour market. Increasing the frequency of moving home automatically increases survival costs. In saying this I am not referring simply to the obvious costs of removal.

A small proportion of full-time employees may, when re-located by their employer, receive some help with removal costs. Any such obligation on the part of the employer does not exist at all in the case of temporary employees. In noting that 'two million houses were bought and sold in 1988' in Britain, Hutton alerts us to a range of potential costs – each house 'requiring new kitchens, bathrooms, curtains and carpets'. Obviously moving home does not *necessarily* generate these costs in all cases. However, as I shall indicate shortly, the costs of refurbishment have become necessary. Less problematic is the fact that 'each transaction required estate agents, banks, building societies, insurance companies, lawyers and architects'.[27]

Employment and its level of remuneration does impact directly on the housing market – hence the marked regional variations in the price of houses. The housing market is especially distorted by particular (local) concentrations of the most affluent, such that a small hovel in a salubrious part of London, for example, attracts a higher purchase price than a spacious, well-appointed property in Liverpool, Newcastle, Manchester or the like. Generally, the most expensive properties of a particular area determine the level of prices for *all* properties in that area. The prices that the vast majority have to pay in purchasing a house are thus inflated by the purchasing power of the affluent.

Now, it can be argued that, in practice, inflated house prices have no relevance to survival costs in so far as people buy in an inflated market at the same time as they are selling. It is assumed that the inflated purchase price is cancelled out by the inflated price received for the property being sold. Mortgage repayments can thus remain at the same level, or as the same proportion of income. This argument, however, is unable to account for the fact that mortgage repayments as a proportion of income, as we have already noted, have increased considerably over the past 20 years. Furthermore, the argument is not applicable across the board. First-time buyers have to pay inflated prices with nothing to sell, and a change of job often means moving to an area where housing is more expensive.

With mortgage repayments as the major item of household expenditure, and in a context in which moving home has become more frequent as a consequence of temporary employment, it becomes necessary to be able to sell quickly in order to minimise the duration of paying for two sets of accommodation costs. Selling a house at a price below its market value may secure a quick sale, but this becomes a realistic option only when the need to cut one's losses becomes urgent. Alternatively, home-owners, more specifically those home-owners that can afford to, are increasingly maintaining and 'improving' their homes to a standard that may enhance, or at least not impede, a quick sale. The new kitchen, new bathroom, or new flooring, for example, will, in some circumstances reflect an unnecessary expenditure on the fashionable. But, for many, these costs, or at least a substantial proportion of them, are more appropriately viewed as necessary.

As employers increasingly reduce their full-time workforce, more and more people will feel obliged to spend on home improvements as part of their preparedness to move elsewhere for employment. The New Right's ideology of a 'flexible workforce' is thus not restricted in its repercussions to the availability of employment and working conditions. It effectively transforms the home from a more or less permanent space to be lived in, into a temporary commodity of continuous investment and reinvestment. And the level of investment in repairs, maintenance and improvements that is required to prevent a reduction in the property's market value is increased both by the inflationary influence of more affluent house buyers and the actual charges of builders.

By this I do not mean that builders themselves overcharge for their work, although many do. Rather I am referring to the greater use of commercial builders rather than neighbours, friends or even cheaper services from the 'underground' economy. People on the move are divorced from neighbourhood networks. Fewer people remain in the same locality long enough to get to know of the cheaper alternatives, or to establish the familiarity and mutual trust with neighbours that enables reciprocal forms of sharing and help. In these circumstances a greater proportion of the population are dispersed into social isolation and anonymity and have to depend on commercial services to address their needs.

It ought to be clear by now that changing labour requirements have a significant impact on escalating survival costs by requiring individuals to adopt new and costlier survival strategies that revolve around an expansion of the sphere of necessary consumption. These extra costs have propelled a majority of the populations of the advanced capitalist societies into debt – mortgages, loans for house repairs, maintenance and improvements, loans for cars, for higher education, for urgent and necessary medical operations, and so on. The interest paid on loans is an obvious source of escalating survival costs. That this interest contributes to the pool of finance capital used for speculative transactions and investment that benefit the already obscenely affluent adds insult to injury.

Changing labour requirements have played havoc with both the distribution of working hours and income. The obvious relevance of this for consumption can be readily discerned. As more people are transferred from a full-time 'job for life' into discontinuous full-time employment interspersed with periods of part-time employment and unemployment, the greater the proportion of the population restricted to little more than the consumption of basic necessities, and the greater the proportion of people seeking cheaper means of survival. For some time now, money and other resources permitting, DIY forms of self-provision have noticeably increased amongst those with time on their hands.[28]

However, this trend, which decreases the total volume of goods that are consumed, is counterbalanced by an opposite trend – inflated working hours amongst those in full-time employment. In the previous chapter the relevance of working hours for the volume of consumption was spelled out. Essentially the longer the working hours the less time (and energy) there is for self-provision, and the greater the need to purchase what one cannot, through lack of time, produce for oneself. Thus lack of time for oneself generates the need for labour-saving devices in the home, for packaged and prepared foods, for fast-food delivery services and so on. These examples are, if you like, the direct effects of a lack of time on consumption. To these we can now add more indirect effects. In particular we can say that the longer the working hours the less time there is for communicating and engaging with others and thus for developing the kinds of social relationships from which co-operative (and free) forms of self-provision emerge.

Even though, throughout the advanced capitalist economies, a full-time job for life is a thing of the past, most people who are in temporary employment do work a full working week *and more.* Because their employment is temporary, and by definition insecure, a variable proportion of their time is taken up with 'showing willing' and 'doing extra' in their jobs in the false hope that they might be retained. Additionally, time is given over to searching for another job, writing letters of application, filling in forms, 'doctoring' CVs, travelling to and attending interviews, and perhaps undergoing a thoroughly useless battery of psychometric tests.[29] And, of course, for many if not all, considerable amounts of time are devoted to transforming their appearance and image (at some cost) into an attractive commodity for the potential employer to purchase.

Considerations such as these illustrate some ways in which changing labour requirements engender insecurities that are addressed by extra purchases and by giving up more time to the employer and to the field of employment in general. There are, however, more ominous trends that contribute directly to inflated working hours. To protect themselves against the insecurities of the labour market increasing numbers of people have drifted into self-employment. A European Commission survey reveals that a majority of those self-employed work in excess of 48 hours a week, and 'are more liable than employed workers to fall below the poverty line'.[30] As Gorz notes, 'the development of self-employment, infinitely "flexible" in all its parameters, is merely the most visible manifestation of the trend towards the abolition of wage-labour'.[31]

The gradual abolition of wage-labour reduces the sphere in which legislation that restricts working hours is applicable. Gorz observes that this trend 'is dominant in the relations between the company and its core workforce'. He continues: 'There it takes the form of the individualization and flexibilization of salaries, the division of the large company into "profit centres" with the employees, as entrepreneurs, responsible for ensuring that profitability is maintained.'[32] Core workers, in this scenario, to protect their own position within the company, collude with their employer's goal of increasing profitability, by working longer hours themselves – indeed these are no longer measured – thereby making other employees redundant, and when convenient, hiring cheap part-time labour. Needless to say, the inflated working hours of core workers decrease time for self-provision, and increase their dependence on commercially provided goods and services.

As we shall see in the next chapter, there are other dimensions to the meaning of inflated working hours that take us into an understanding of consumption that is even further removed from that provided by the ideology of consumerism. Enough has been said here, however, to indicate that the explanation for increasing levels of individual consumption, amongst a majority in the advanced capitalist societies, is best pursued in considerations that are afforded no space in the ideology of consumerism.

The reasons for increasing consumption in the advanced capitalist societies, the latest ideology of consumerism would have us believe, are to be found in all the ways in which consumers find consumption to be irresistably attractive. It is assumed that people can afford, by dint of their growing affluence, to buy what they cannot resist. In sharp contrast to this view I have emphasised that: first, only a quarter of the populations of the advanced capitalist societies are affluent enough to regularly indulge themselves in consumerism. Second, incomes for the majority have not kept pace with increases in survival costs. This means that an increasing proportion of income is taken up with escalating survival costs. And third, escalating survival costs derive from having to pay more for some basic necessities, and from an expansion of the number of goods and services that qualify as basic necessities. This expansion has been brought about by social changes that ensure that survival needs can be addressed only in complex and circuitous ways.

Part Three

Consumption, Capitalism and Post-capitalism

7   Consumption for What?

Up to now my main concern has been that of *explaining* individual consumption. This has been a theoretical exercise involving a critical assessment of the most popular explanation of consumerism followed by the altogether different theory of consumption presented in Part Two. The continuing, and indeed growing, significance of survival needs, as opposed to post-necessity values, in accounting for most of what most people consume has been emphasised. Needless to say, this emphasis does paint a picture of the advanced capitalist societies that radically departs from that portrayed in the latest ideology of consumerism. Whether or not governments, and their policy advisers, are aware of the extent to which the lives of a majority of their populace are dominated by the imperative of 'making ends meet' is a matter of speculation. I suspect that they are.

What is clear is that governments know that electoral success or failure, for the most part, turns on whether or not a majority feel that they are getting better or worse off financially. All governments of the advanced capitalist societies, unless their term of office coincides with a recession, can point to annual increases in consumer spending, and in the volume of goods consumed, and unhesitatingly declare that these increases are signs of a healthy economy. They are thus assumed to be signs indicating that people are not only getting better off but will continue to do so. Yet, the experience of the majority contradicts this. The evidence presented in the previous chapter demonstrates that since the mid-1970s most people are actually worse off in the sense that survival costs take up an increasing proportion of their incomes. Yes, people are consuming more and spending more but for reasons that cannot be construed in terms of a growing affluence.

When increases in consumer spending are attributable to increases in the cost of survival, and when increases in the volume of goods consumed is attributable to the need to regularly replace 'durable' basic necessities for example, the economy is obviously not as healthy as we are led to believe. The 'feel good' factor associated with free spending has a limited applicability, that is, it may exist amongst the most affluent minority and for those with a temporary upturn in their fortunes. And when our experience contradicts the constant message that everybody is better off, individuals, especially those existing in relative isolation, are encouraged to blame themselves for being unable to share in the growing prosperity.

Increasing spending and consumption, for a majority, does not result in a corresponding improvement to their lives, but it does benefit the capitalist system. Increases in incomes have got swallowed up, mainly in housing and transport costs, including the costs of interest on loans. What is earned from the capitalist system in wages is grabbed back by the very same system in necessary spending on imposed costs. Employment, which is increasingly experienced as an imposition, provides an income that is increasingly used to pay out for these imposed costs.

Does this make sense? From the viewpoint of the individual it makes little sense – working at a senseless job in order to pay for senseless survival costs. The individual is caught in a vicious circle, and kept there for fear of putting survival in jeopardy. It is this fear, which in concrete terms is the fear of being unable to pay the mortgage or the car loan, and in turn the fear of loss of employment, that disciplines the free individual into a pragmatic compliance with a senseless system.

This is not to say that individuals do not want to be better off. Of course they do. Being better off financially has become *the only way* of surviving, of experiencing a comfort zone beyond survival that enables relief from the pressures of survival, and of being able to afford the little and not so little treats that offer some compensation for *a life that has to be sold in order to live.*

Given the stranglehold that the capitalist system exercises over the means and conditions of survival, is there any wonder that wanting to be better off becomes a dominant orientation ordering our practical lives? As such it can lead only to wanting to consume more and better. Wanting to be better off is a wanting that derives from and is imposed by the circumstances in which we live – circumstances prescribed, controlled and manipulated by the capitalist system. A little more money is never enough to alter radically this state of affairs unless 'the more' is massively more, as in a huge lottery or pools win.

As I have emphasised we should not equate this with people *voluntarily* adopting the model of the 'good life' prescribed by capitalism, in which our only aspirations are those that are channelled into consumption and in which more consumption means greater happiness. We are *materially manipulated* to fit this model by circumstances beyond our control. We are entrapped in a system, the consumer society, that closes off practical alternatives, a system into which we are conscripted as individuals to play the only game in town. Failure to participate in the game condemns the individual to total deprivation. But participation in the game does not guarantee the avoidance of deprivation. There are winners and losers. For the majority *luck* (ideologically translated into merit – a mixture of effort and 'ability'), more than anything else, determines individual success or failure. For many, to make one's own luck in order to increase the chances of success requires nothing less than transforming one's self into an absurd commodity form to be sold to an impressed employer.

Yet the evidence of life-satisfaction studies consistently reveals that a majority of people's wants are not exhausted by wanting to consume more. Indeed, as I noted in Chapter 4, after survival, people want to prioritise values that have absolutely nothing to do with consumption. Wanting a more meaningful and satisfying life typically translates into wanting more autonomy, stable, loving relationships, good friends and so on. Having to sell one's life to live, for many, impedes the living of a meaningful and satisfying life. And this is surely senseless.

The senselessness of 'consumer society', its irrationality, provides the focus for much of this chapter. In particular I will emphasise, contrary to the rhetoric of governments competing for national advantage in a global capitalist system, that the senselessness of consumer society has its source in profit-driven wealth creation. The whole world is ruled by big capital, and it is precisely because individual governments do compete with each other to gain favour from big capital, that they adopt policies that reinforce and extend the senselessness of consumer society.

The sources of wealth, essentially human labour and natural resources, under capitalism, I shall argue, have been and are being used to develop a consumer society that makes survival a lottery (especially in the Third World but increasingly in the First World) that undermines autonomy, the true basis of a better quality of life, and that abuses the environment in ways that threaten the survival and autonomy of future generations.

My argument is intended to expose the urgent need for the human world to control democratically and begin to abolish capitalism. It is not intended to lend weight to those voices, typically the voices of well-intentioned social-democratic politicians, expressing a need for capitalism to reform itself, to save itself from its own greed. Capitalism has been around long enough; it has had plenty of time to reform itself, and it has consistently demonstrated that it is incapable of self-reform, at least in ways that benefit humankind and the environment.

Some radicals argue that a start can be made in this direction if *individuals* in consumer societies begin to restrict their consumption. I shall discuss the limitations of this strategy, and argue that it is the *institutional* consumption of capitalism itself that most requires restricting. This can be achieved, without material deprivation, as an outcome of expanding autonomy. I shall argue, however, that the expansion of autonomy can be attained only by an effective challenge to the capitalist system's control of the means and conditions of survival. The kinds of policies most likely to constitute this challenge do necessitate, amongst other things, an entirely different role for the state – a role that takes us back to conceptual-isations of the state as embodying the will and authority of the people rather than the servant of capital. The subordination of nation-states to the power of global capital provides a useful starting point in helping us make sense of the senselessness of the consumer society.

Capital and State

What from the viewpoint of the individual is senseless, is, from the viewpoint of the capitalist system an ideal arrangement – an arrange-ment that governments can applaud in the name of a healthily functioning economy, and an arrangement that delivers profits for the capitalist class. Consumption is at the centre of this arrangement. It is *the* way of life imposed by the capitalist system, but promoted as unproblematically identical with what we want. The best way to get what we want, we are often reminded, is to allow the wealth creators (the capitalist class!) free rein. Their wealth-creating practices, we are told, will lead to more and better-paid jobs.

But as we have seen the so-called wealth-creating practices, especially in recent times, come at a cost – financial and existential costs for the individual and environmental costs. At the same time governments, led by the examples set by the US and Britain, attempt to attract wealth-creators, by offering major companies subsidies and other inducements such as tax breaks (most transnational companies *do not* pay tax on profits) and low tax on the personal incomes of the wealthy.[1] As a consequence governments have either to reduce public spending or fund it through disproportionately high taxation on the incomes of the majority, and increasing other forms of tax, such as purchase tax (VAT), road tax, property tax and so on.

Reductions in public spending have been achieved by opening up areas of public provision to private entrepreneurship. This has invariably resulted in poorer and more expensive services. In spite of overwhelming evidence that this is so, let alone the commonsense knowledge that private profit and public service are contradictory, governments peddle the myth of efficiency to justify the extension of free market notions of accountability into areas, for example caring (health care, child care, residential care, social services) and education, for which it is totally irrelevant.

Accounting, as in 'doing the accounts', is fundamentally an arithmetical and quantifying process. Certain activities, like love, caring, communication, thinking and so on, cannot be quantified, and cannot thus be treated as commodities with a price, an exchange-value expressed in quantifiable terms. It makes no sense at all to talk about 'consuming' these kinds of activities. Money cannot buy them because they cannot be bought, and they cannot be bought because they cannot be priced (measured) in monetary terms.

While the emphasis on 'value for money' does reflect an inappropriate consumerist approach toward education and caring services, it typically translates into a focus on those aspects of these services that can be counted – teacher–pupil ratios, the percentage of children falling below a nationally prescribed standard of literacy and numeracy for their age group, the length of hospital waiting lists, the length of time patients have to wait for operations, the number of hospital beds and so on. Value for money thus bears no relation to the essence of the *quality* of education and caring. As funding for the education and health service depends on these services meeting value for money targets, they inevitably invent and give priority to funding-oriented practices. As a consequence education and health professionals are increasingly involved in practices that are irrelevant to the needs that they are supposed to address.

When public opinion expresses a strong dissatisfaction with education and health provision, so strong that the future electoral success of a government might be in jeopardy, politicians attempt to appease the public in the only way they know by throwing a little more money at the failing services. At best this can only help to shore up services that are failing precisely because under-funding in the past has spawned a 'professional' culture devoid of good will and the kind of concern for children and patients that expresses itself in a genuine commitment to the well-being of both.

In these circumstances, vividly in evidence in Britain, massive amounts of money would be required to stop the rot. A doubling in the numbers of teachers and health professionals, with the supporting material infrastructure, might enable the education and health services to break with the habits that have arisen in response to under-funding, and begin to develop professional cultures dedicated to the development of human potential on the one hand, and to patients' health on the other.

Governments rule out a massive injection of funds into failing public services – it would send alarm bells ringing amongst big capital. And smaller injections of funds are 'talked up', their significance exaggerated, for the ears of the public. The capitalist class is assured that the money will come from the sale of state assets or from savings in state expenditure elsewhere. The public are reminded that extra spending on education and health will have to deliver 'value for taxpayers' money', and the capitalist class knows that this means even more business-style accountability. 'Boosted' with insufficient injections of cash that are targeted at providing more of the very same that is already failing, the education and health services inevitably get further distanced from the needs they are intended to serve.

Giving taxpayers value for their money has become a slogan for the very opposite. It is part and parcel of the double-speak that governments engage in to conceal the transfer of wealth from the majority to the wealthy minority. Some governments (again those of the US and Britain have led the way), promote tax cuts in the name of enhancing personal incomes. When the tax cuts result in poorer and more expensive public provision the majority are the losers. If, for example, a government decides not to build a public library, and announces that the £600 million saved will constitute a saving for the tax payer, and if it then (to prove its point) distributes this £600 million equally (which it never does) among its population of let us say 60 million people, each person would receive £10 to spend as they will. Access to thousands of books is denied, but the individual might be able to buy *one* book. Such is the logic and senselessness of a society in which the public (and the public good) is reduced to a market place of commodities for individual purchase. Needs, once addressed through public provision, can go unsatisfied altogether. But we *might* have a little more money that cannot in any way address these needs or reduce the burden of other needs.

In opening up societies to the dictates of big capital, nation-states have effectively reduced their sphere of sovereignty, and in siding with big capital they are treading a path that can only store up problems that they would rather not face. Some idea of what lays ahead can be discerned from the consequences of the profit-making strategies currently being adopted by big business.

Profit, Incomes and Consumption

The search for ever-increasing profits, in recent times, has propelled individual enterprises toward a radical reduction in labour costs. This is achieved in a number of ways – relocating the enterprise in a country where labour costs are considerably lower, cutting the labour force and lowering wages. But what might make sense in terms of increasing profitability from the viewpoint of the individual enterprise, might, if pursued by all major companies, make very little sense for capitalism as a whole. The continuing reduction of labour costs does reduce the income available for consumption. Profitability achieved by lowering labour costs is thus undermined by the loss of profits from consumption for capitalism as a whole. As Greider puts it: 'the global system is astride a great fault line. The wondrous new technologies and globalizing strategies are able to produce an abundance of goods, but fail to generate the consumer incomes sufficient to buy them.'[2]

In truth, capitalism has always operated with far fewer consumers than there are people. Those without incomes are obviously of no benefit to capitalism as consumers but are nevertheless useful in depressing wages. But the labour costs reduction strategies that are being adopted, as noted in the previous chapter, reveal a direction, the ultimate destination of which is self-destructive for capitalism. While capitalism does its best to claw back the incomes of all consumers, it has always been most interested in producing for the most affluent, who, after all, have money in excess of need. But as the distribution of incomes falls into a marked division between a very affluent minority and the rest, producing for the most affluent becomes increasingly important.

While in theory it is of no consequence to companies how many consumers buy their products so long as they are sold for a handsome profit, in practice the most affluent are limited as a market. One might own several houses and umpteen cars, but one cannot live in more than one house or drive more than one car at any one time. The accumulative effect of what makes sense from the short-term viewpoint of individual companies competing for a profitable market share, is that the capitalist sytem will undermine itself. The affluent will be feeding off themselves. Greider explains:

> ... when rising incomes are broadly distributed, it creates mass purchasing power – the rising demand that fuels a virtuous cycle of growth, savings and new investment. When incomes are narrowly distributed, as they are now, the economic system feeds upon itself, eroding its own energies for expansion, burying consumers and business, even governments, in impossible accumulations of debt. A relative few become fabulously wealthy, but a healthy economy is not sustained by manic investing. Nothing about modern technologies or the 'information age' has altered these ancient fundamentals.[3]

The 'manic investing' to which Greider refers is largely focused on making profits in the richest of all casinos – the stock market – on the basis of transactions that deliver *individual wealth*, but are cut off from wealth *production*. This is a trend that serves no social purpose, other than subordinating all societies to the uncertainties of a lottery in which the big prizes have already been claimed. Gorz sees this very clearly. He tells us that 'financial logic is winning out over economic logic ... Financial power, referred to euphemistically as "the market", is becoming independent of societies and the real economy, and is imposing its norms of profitability on businesses and states.'[4]

Gorz is merely stating what is common knowledge amongst the controllers of financial capital. He cites an influential Bundesbank president, who, in 1996 stated that 'The financial markets will increasingly play the role of "policemen" ... Politicians have to understand that they are now under the control of the financial markets and not, any longer, of national debates.'[5]

Capitalism, then, is pursuing a direction that is beginning to eat into 'the health' of the economies of the advanced capitalist societies. Nation-states in the First World, that once controlled their own economies, now find themselves having to 'suck up' to global capital. This, of course, has long been the experience of Third World societies. Talk of Third World conditions, as for example in certain public services, in urban decay, in social exclusion, or in social disintegration more generally, creeping into First World societies is no longer confined to the more radical and critical voices. The division between the most affluent and the majority of the populations *within* the advanced capitalist societies, has, over the past 30 years, begun to mirror the longer established trend of global inequalities, and the marked division of wealth within Third World societies.

In one fundamental sense, however, the globalisation of capital and its growing power reveals more clearly than ever that the uncontrolled pursuit of profit-driven wealth creation radicalises the contradiction between capital and labour. Nowhere is this more evident than in the Third World societies where the use, abuse and disposal of labour to suit the convenience of profit has a long history. It is in the Third World, far more so than in the First World, that we can see the human costs of wealth creation geared toward producing for the most affluent. And it is in the Third World that we get a glimpse of the First World of the future.

Disposable People

Elizabeth Dore has pointed out that 'in 1890, Europe was twice as wealthy (per capita) as China or India. By 1940, it was forty times richer; in 1990, it was seventy times richer.'[6] Statistics of this kind, with a few temporary exceptions, are to be found across the globe. They are the direct results of that form of imperialism known as colonialism, and in 'post-colonial' times of the imperialism of an international capitalist class. In essence, from the viewpoint of the capitalist class the Third World is one massive source of profit.

I do not intend to provide a detailed analysis of the way in which the Third World has been, and continues to be, impoverished. I merely want to establish that capitalism has a long history of destroying human life, and that it is unrealistic to expect it to voluntarily change its ways.

Colonialism had already prepared the ground for modern capitalism. Food-abundant, self-sufficient societies organised around local needs and with the foresight to maintain ecological balance were reduced, initially by the power of the gun, into non-societies that were, for the colonial masters, essentially physical spaces full of resources (land, raw materials, including the raw material otherwise known as 'humans') to be appropriated for their own use. Whether in the interests of domination or profit, or both, what had evolved over centuries, for example, local democracies and culturally-based divisions of space, were swept away. In spite of this people were able to muster an ongoing resistance to colonial rule and almost everywhere eventually achieved political independence.

Almost everywhere the political elites of newly independent nations attempted to impose a model of development borrowed from the advanced capitalist societies, in heavy industry, manufacturing and agriculture. At the same time major cities were re-built to resemble the prestige cities of their former colonisers, at least with respect to grand buildings, hotels, airports and other images of affluence. All of this 'development' cost money that most countries just did not have. No problem. It was borrowed from First World banks and nations. Aping many of the standard business practices of capitalism, it was no surprise that varying proportions of borrowed money found its way into corrupt hands. But, especially in Africa, huge amounts of borrowed money went into the development of armies to deal with conflicts within and between 'nations' that had been created by colonial powers. In carving up the continent between them, the colonialists had totally ignored centuries-old culturally-based boundaries between societies. This proved to be highly lucrative for the producers and suppliers of armaments.

Most Third World countries quickly found themselves having to obtain more loans in order to pay off existing loans. New loans came with more stringent conditions. 'Development', already distorted by unequal terms of trade with First World companies and by the devaluation of Third World currencies, took on a much narrower meaning centred on the need to earn foreign currency to relieve debt. By and large this has entailed a more intensive industrialisation of agriculture controlled by major transnational companies to supply First World markets, and a scramble for 'inward' investment. The latter translates into offering transnational companies favourable conditions, such as low wage costs, subsidies (backhanders), no tax on profits and so on, to set up and stay.

As the involvement of transnational companies in the Third World has expanded, 'development' has been further distorted. It is well and truly an underdevelopment involving the harnessing of industrial and agricultural production to serve affluent markets. This underdevelopment is controlled by transnational companies, and the institutions of world governance, supported where necessary by internal and external forces of repression.

In the meantime more underdevelopment is available with the help of loans made necessary by the impoverishment imposed by earlier 'development' itself. Dore notes that 'together, Latin American, African and Asian countries pay about three times more every year just in payments to service foreign debt than the total they receive in development assistance through all channels'. She comments that 'these debt payments are, in essence, a forced contribution from the world's poor to the world's wealthy countries'.[7]

Recently there have been 'debt relief' initiatives launched by the World Bank and IMF. To qualify for debt relief (and additional loans) poor countries have to subject themselves to the rigours (referred to ideologically as 'reforms') of a Structural Adjustment Programme (SAP). This involves, amongst other things, the privatisation of state-owned industries and services, deregulation and anything else that will reduce public spending, with the exception of spending on the military and police. Spending on the latter is 'necessary' to ensure the repression of the civil strife anticipated as a consequence of the SAP.

Paul Donovan correctly observes that 'the reality of the SAP for Third World countries' is 'the ceding of a large amount of their sovereignty to the IMF and the World Bank to run the country'. The 'overall effect of the SAP' he continues, 'is to drive already poor people into increasingly desperate poverty, whilst opening up the assets of the indebted countries for transnational corporations to exploit'.[8] The evidence supporting these effects is staggering. In the richest part of Zambia, for example, between 1993 and 1999, the mortality rates of children under five doubled, and the life expectancy of adults fell from 54.4 to 42.6 years.

People already existing at a sub-survival level are experiencing even more austerity now – school fees, doctor and hospital fees, more expensive basic necessities as a consequence of the forced withdrawal of state subsidies – for the false promise of a prosperous tomorrow. Tomorrow, in reality, reveals the truth of development – further impoverishment and death for the peoples sacrificed for the most affluent. Susan George sums up the reality of development for the poor by drawing on an example of Peruvian humour.

OFFICIAL: You'll have to tighten your belt.
CITIZEN: I can't. I ate it yesterday.[9]

The truth of development reveals a fundamental truth about capitalism: *capitalism is run by the affluent for the affluent*. That a small minority of others may derive some benefits from being used by capitalists and that there may be some positive social consequences emanating from capitalism does not falsify this truth. Whenever and wherever it suits, capitalism will stop at nothing to realise its profits. If profit means that masses of people must die then so be it. The relationship between capitalism and the Third World is living proof of this. The only basis for arguing otherwise is *racist*.

In other words some might argue, in private if not publicly, that capitalism's exploitation of the Third World is legitimate in the sense that the populations of the Third World are not part of humanity, that they do not really count as people and can thus be used to enrich humanity proper. Such a white supremacist ideology can be found amongst those who believe that the abuse of Third World peoples could not possibly be mirrored in the 'home' countries of the international capitalist class.

Of course a racism is implicated in the way in which capitalism does not value Third World lives, but before we get carried away with this train of thought, let us not forget that in the home of capitalism, the very same disregard for human life that capitalism displays toward Third World populations, has a very long history. Let us not forget that this disregard is not restricted to immigrants, refugees and asylum seekers – it has always impacted on the indigenous working class. In spite of over a century of struggle by organised labour, as recently as the late 1970s employers' advertisements for hands, not people, not even workers or labourers, appeared in local newspapers in Britain. And just a few years later the government of the day (a most pleasing and obedient government for big business) gleefully swept away many of workers' hard-won rights, and terminated a lengthy strike in the coal industry by unashamedly starving miners back to work.

The truth of the matter is that the blind pursuit of profit is essentially colour-blind. This is not to say that big business is non-racist, but it is to say that when it comes to making profit the colour of those to be exploited and abused is rarely a consideration. The exploited, regardless of colour, are nothing more than potential assets or raw materials to be costed. They are treated, in practice, as if they are outside of humanity. The right to exploit is reserved for those who qualify for humanity – the international capitalist class!

The 'right' to exploit and to condemn millions of people to impoverishment and early deaths is much easier to exercise in the Third World than in the First World, but this does not prevent big business from discarding those, in the advanced capitalist societies, that are surplus to their requirements. Workers' rights, let alone human rights can be circumvented or brushed aside when it suits profitability. Human rights, as represented in the United Nations Universal Declaration of Human Rights in 1948, are rarely made to count in the face of business interests. C.B. Macpherson notes that 'businessmen are sceptical or hostile, seeing human rights as the thin edge of a wedge that is being driven into the historic rights of private enterprise and market freedoms'.[10]

Herein resides another truth: the 'rights' that form the ideological basis of capitalism take precedence over all other rights. Indeed it is somewhat bizarre that the unwillingness of the IMF to advance loans to particular countries is often justified (as if the IMF has to justify anything) on the grounds that these countries have poor human rights records. This is the very same IMF that *requires* a blatant violation of human rights as a condition of receiving loans. Only the most dehumanised and anti-human can make such demands.

It is evident that it is the most powerful agents of capital, blindly captivated by the demons of profit, that are outside of and against humanity. How else can one interpret the stock market slump on Friday 8 March 1996 at the news that a record 705,000 jobs had been created in the US in February of that year? A fall in unemployment figures does mean that more people can improve their survival prospects. But for the controllers of financial capital it means the possibility of reduced profits.

> The markets which mainly fear overheating and inflation were victims of real panic ... On Wall Street the Dow Jones index, which had already broken records on Tuesday, plummeted more than 3 per cent ... European markets also fell steeply ... The financial markets seem particularly vulnerable to *any bad news*.[11]

The anti-humans, it would seem, would prefer to restrict the numbers of humans entering their world.

Disposable Environment

The brazen genocidal policies of the most powerful agents of capital are complemented by, and in many respects enable, their cavalier approach to finite resources, renewable resources and pollution. For some time now ecologists have warned that producing for high levels of consumption in the advanced capitalist societies and the consequences of affluent consumption are destroying the ecological balance of the planet. The language of environmental degradation – the depletion of natural resources, health-threatening pollution, global warming, genetically modified food and so on – is an increasingly familiar one. It is more than familiar, too, to the international capitalist class.

The rationality of profit promotes a dangerous irrationality in relation to the mounting evidence of environmental destruction at the hands of capitalism. That industrial production is polluting, for example, is both denied and fully accepted! In the face of local opposition to the polluting effects of industrial production in the advanced capitalist societies major companies typically deny any responsibility. They will even go so far as to pay their own team of 'neutral' scientists to conclude that there is insufficient evidence, or even no evidence at all, to link their industrial practices with the 'alleged' polluting effects. They *know* that what they vigorously deny is in fact the truth. For at the very same time as they are fighting their fraudulant case, they are buying time to eke out more profits and to prepare to move their polluting production, as thousands of others have done before them, to the Third World. Here, where pollution controls and health and safety regulations are lax or non-existent in order to attract transnational companies, industrial production can proceed without the inconvenient interruptions of green protestors. Furthermore, exporting pollution to the Third World does reduce the health risks within the environments in which almost all of the international capitalist class and their families live.

The fact that pollution, wherever its source, is *ultimately* global in its effects, is of little relevance. Profits *now* are of far greater importance. And it is this that underpins the absence of qualms about using up resources in the production of consumer goods. The urge to make profit is sufficient to override any concern that certain resources – oil, aluminium, copper, iron, mercury, nickel, tin and zinc for example – are predicted to run out in the forseeable future. Besides, is it not the case, some argue, that these predictions have proved to be alarmist? Take the case of oil. Do we not keep on discovering new oil fields? And, even if the most alarmist predictions were true, it is argued, man has always come up with something. Science and technology will come to the rescue.

This kind of argument is seriously flawed. If a heavy smoker was told by a doctor that death from smoking was most probable within the next ten years unless the habit was stopped immediately, and if the smoker continued to smoke, arguing that medical science was bound to come up with something to keep him alive, his argument would be dismissed by any rational person as utter nonsense. Likewise when reserves of vital resources are known to be limited, it makes little sense to use them as if they were limitless. The profit motive is sufficiently powerful in some quarters to render the otherwise rational into the blindly irrational.

The folly of the dominance of the profit motive is clearly exposed in the case of 'renewable' resources, such as air, water and land. Industrialised agriculture has developed to the point where it is totally dependent on costly heavy machinery, pesticides, fertilisers and non-renewable sources of energy – it takes three tons of oil to produce one ton of fertiliser. Industrialised agriculture in its most developed form is unsustainable in the sense that it destroys the soil, poisons water and the food chain, and uses up finite energy resources. In the US alone over one-third of the topsoil has been irretrievably lost. Pesticides kill natural predators, but these have been replaced by creatures that have developed resistance to the chemicals used. Ever more chemical 'solutions' are created, and so the inevitable cycle of chemical-zapping and resistance goes on, and with it the growing cocktail of poisons entering the food chain.

Whatever the environmental, health and nutritional costs of the most advanced forms of industrialised agriculture, the benefits in terms of crop yields and profits have been temporarily evident. However, what proved to be an 'efficient' form of food production in the North American context has been extended to the Third World with far less success. The most fertile lands in the Third World have long been used to grow crops (cash crops) to feed the 'developed' tastes of the First World. What began as plantation agriculture under colonial rule has been developed into a fine art under agribusiness. Prevented from growing for their own needs, Third World countries export cash crops, such as tea, cocoa, coffee, cheaply to the First World at prices controlled by major companies, and are forced to buy expensive imported food for their own people. From the viewpoint of capitalism this makes perfect sense. Quite simply profit is increased by this arrangement, and additionally there are opportunities for more profit from the transportation, storage, processing, preservation and packaging of food.

Transnational companies control more than just cash crops. They actually produce, at great cost, some of what people once produced for themselves, and employ contracted farmers for the same purpose. Contracted farmers are required to use seeds, pesticides and fertilisers provided, at a price, by the controlling transnational company. Fewer local farmers can afford to participate in contracted work and are increasingly having to sell their land in order to survive. But the drive to extract more profit from the land, given the chemically intensive nature of the agricultural methods used, depletes the soil of its nutrients, and through erosion, compromises even more than is currently the case: the survival prospects of future generations. The problem of soil erosion is exacerbated by forest clearance and by small farmers being forced, for reasons of immediate survival, to over-farm the less fertile soil to which they are restricted.

A Note on the Ideology of Development

It ought to be clear by now that the kind of lies that we have been fed by the ideologues of big business with regard to their humanitarian motives for 'civilising' the world are nothing more than crude ideology. 'Civilisation' for big business means the imposition of a model of 'development', the cutting edge of which is the kind of 'society' best represented by the US. Critics of this model are justified in adopting the stance of 'say no more'.

But let us note that the 'developed' societies are so-called primarily because of their wealth which is materialised in a social and physical environment that has artificially generated high levels of consumption. This model of development, held up as the ideal for all to follow, not only represents an impoverished view of civilisation, but it can be pursued only at the expense of the environment, and *only by ensuring underdevelopment elsewhere.*

In other words, the level of development attained in the advanced capitalist societies *cannot* be attained everywhere. That development has been attained only by the most *powerful* (militarily and economically) nations appropriating a disproportionate share of global resources. The US, for example, with only 4 per cent of the world's population, consumes 25 per cent of the world's annual oil production.

It has been calculated that if Africa were to be developed to the point attained in the US, its energy requirements alone would surpass the current annual global consumption of oil, and would radically increase global pollution, including greenhouse gas pollution. (It would, however, reduce the proportion of global greenhouse gas emissions for which the US is responsible – not that this concerns the US government.) The truth of the matter is that western-style development was never intended for all societies.

The ideologues promoting western-style development as *the* global model for all societies to follow *know* that this model is not viable, though they will not publicly admit it. It would hardly do for the 'respectable' institutions of world governance to admit that the role of resource-rich Third World countries is that of enabling more wealth to accrue to the affluent, or to admit that unbridled capitalism wreaks environmental havoc. They cannot admit that famine in the Third World is a consequence of development, and that their solution (there is no alternative!) to the problem of feeding the world will create more famine. They cannot admit that their solution is not necessary to alleviate hunger, but it is necessary to maintain profitability.

Susan George exposes the hypocrisy of the 'humanitarianism' that provides a gloss to disguise the real interests of transnational agribusiness.

> I could prove to you with simple arithmetic that if 15 million children are now dying from hunger every year, they could be saved with less than a two-thousandth of the world's harvests (0.002 per cent), even assuming you gave them an adult ration and that there was absolutely no food available to them locally – not even breast milk.[12]

Up to now the international capitalist class has been able to point to the obvious benefits of consumer comforts available to First World populations as sufficient 'justification' for anti-Third World and anti-environmental practices. But as profit-making becomes more manic this justification will appease fewer people. The 'good life' of more consumption is also the bad life of deteriorating environmental conditions, traffic congestion, worsening health and safety standards, nutritionless food, insecure employment, increasing survival costs, declining public services, urban decay, social disintegration and so on. We are forced to participate in this bad life in order to survive. The inflated price we have to pay to survive benefits the very ones that have been most instrumental in creating the bad life and ensures that we are beholden to them in the search for jobs.

We are heading toward a scenario, some might argue that we are already there, in which an international capitalist class, through greed alone, rules a network of enclaves of capitalism that are increasingly irrelevant to what people most need. These enclaves have no other purpose than to increase profits for the capitalist class. While 'selected' workers may occupy permanent or, increasingly, temporary positions within these enclaves, enabling a fuller participation as consumers, from the viewpoint of the capitalist class they are labour resources to be used and discarded. Profit alone dictates their disposable use. This is progress!

The Need to Reduce Affluent Consumption

The devastating environmental and human consequences of systems of production geared toward producing for high levels of affluent consumption are of growing concern to an increasing number of people. For several years now there has been a steady proliferation of ecologically informed protest groups, and more recently, anti-capitalist groups have emerged. Television coverage of anti-capitalist demonstrations has been mixed. On the one hand there has been a disproportionate focus on violent protest (as if smashing windows of banks, overturning luxury cars, and skirmishes with armed police are in the same league as the murderous machine known as capitalism), but on the other hand there have been attempts, if limited, to convey the sources of people's anger with the capitalist system. What we rarely get, however, is coverage of the range of currently debated proposals for saving the environment and the Third World, and for developing a post-capitalist future.

The most radical critics of capitalism are agreed that the survival of the global population, now and in the future, will require a significant reduction in the volume of consumption in the advanced capitalist societies. In fact this is understating things somewhat. It would be more accurate to say that consumer-based lifestyles will have to go. The strategies proposed for achieving this are numerous. But unsurprisingly, given the predominance of the ideology of individualism, the need to reduce consumption is invariably taken to mean that the principal strategy for achieving this is that of urging individuals to consume less. Furthermore, this kind of strategy is often advocated by some radical critics of capitalism as a strategy that can begin to make a difference as of now. The voluntary self-limitation of consumption, in this view, is seen as the way forward to a post-capitalist future.

I want to make it clear that there is an urgent need to reduce the volume of consumption in the advanced capitalist societies. Consistent with the arguments presented throughout this book, the strategies most likely to achieve this are those that can effectively address the causes of inflated consumption. These causes, I have argued, are not to be found within individuals, but reside within the structural features of the developed capitalist societies. It would thus seem to make most sense to direct our energies into those strategies intended to deliver systemic (rather than individual) change. To reinforce this view I will initially consider the limitations of a strategy of voluntary self-limitation prior to discussing more relevant strategies.

Voluntary Self-limitation?

It ought to be clear from the arguments presented in Part Two that a policy centred on urging individuals to consume less will have a limited appeal unless there are structural and systemic changes that enable individuals to experience voluntary self-limitation as beneficial, rather than as a recipe for deprivation. It also ought to be clear that by this I do not mean that people are personally so wedded to consumption, for reasons of pleasure, meaning or identity, that they could not possibly consume less. People are locked into high levels of consumption for reasons not of their own choosing.

Of course the most affluent 25 per cent have the capacity, if not the desire, to significantly reduce their personal consumption. But this capacity, that is the capacity for unnecessary consumption, is shrinking for the majority, and for the poor it just does not exist. There is no harm in advocating that we choose to buy the least elaborate of basic necessities and that we stop buying things that we do not need. And there is certainly no harm in promoting energy conservation, reduced water consumption, the re-cycling of household waste and so on. But even if everyone adopted such strategies, the problems that environmentally friendly and 'ethical' forms of consumption are intended to alleviate would still remain. The real problem is that development, in its most progressed form, has generated social conditions in which survival itself has come to depend on the consumption of an expanding range of goods and services, and thus on increasing survival costs.

Sure enough, most basic necessities come in several forms, from the simple to the elaborate, from the very basic to the very grand, from the relatively cheap to the extremely expensive, and so forth. This merely means that *there are choices within necessity*. We do not choose necessity – that is an absurdity. Nor do we choose the social environment that determines what counts as basic necessities. Nor, for the most part and for most of us, do we choose our level of income that determines our capacity for choosing how we satisfy our survival needs. While we can, for example, choose to drive a more fuel-efficient, smaller car instead of a more environmentally unfriendly, larger car, we are still driving a car. In circumstances where employment and employability are dependent on 'flexible mobility', the ownership of a car is a necessity. To choose not to own a car, in these circumstances, is to choose deprivation. Who in their right mind would choose deprivation?

It is evident that a strategy of voluntary self-limitation, in our present circumstances, will inevitably be perceived by a growing number of people as self-inflicted deprivation to add to the experience of socially created and imposed deprivation. And I am not just referring to 'relative deprivation' in which deprivation is defined in relation to some standard of non-deprivation, such as, for example, an income less than half the median income. By deprivation I am referring to the on-going experience of being unable to address sufficiently *all* survival needs, and thus having to prioritise those survival needs requiring urgent attention. This experience is a permanent one for a minority, and for the majority the periods of temporary relief from deprivation are becoming fewer. It is increasingly common to have to make choices between replacing the car or repairing the roof, for example, or lower down the income scale, of paying the electricity bill or buying shoes for the children.

Socially imposed deprivation in the advanced capitalist societies arises in the main from the inability of these societies to enable *all* of its citizens access to the resources necessary for the sufficient satisfaction of *all* survival needs. Society has failed to keep up with the monster of progress. This failure is inextricably bound up with the developed social conditions in which we have to survive. For it is the exploitation of these conditions, our social environment, by financial capital and big business, that is primarily and predominantly responsible for the high levels of consumption in these societies, by *ensuring* that survival itself is dependent on inflated consumption and its attendant debt.

People know this well. To reduce consumption to a level that will be beneficial for the environment, Third World populations *and* the majority in the First World will require radical changes to the means and conditions of survival in the advanced capitalist societies. But while present conditions prevail, and in the absence of collective solutions in which individuals might place their hopes and energies, people will continue to pursue individual, consumer-based, solutions to the problem of survival. These solutions should not be seen as freely chosen, an assumption implied in the strategy of voluntary self-limitation, but as practical responses to circumstances over which individuals, acting individually, have no control.

Institutional Consumption

Voluntary self-limitation in consumption is limited as a strategy for reducing consumption because it mis-identifies the sources and principal *site* of over-consumption. What we, as individuals, consume has already been *institutionally consumed*, often several times over. Institutional consumption is the main site of consumption. I shall make clear what I mean by this in due course, and in doing so it will become evident that institutional consumption accounts for a far greater proportion of the total volume of goods consumed than the sum total of what is consumed individually and domestically. It is institutional consumption, not individual consumption, that is primarily responsible for inflated survival costs and ecological demands.

Institutional consumption is essentially of two types: consumption by the institutions of capitalism, and public consumption. The latter, which has typically involved the state in purchasing and maintaining roads, hospitals, schools, prisons, airports, military equipment and establishments and so on, accounts for approximately 50 per cent of all consumption throughout Western Europe. The concept of public consumption is useful in so far as it indicates a site of consumption that cannot be construed as individual or domestic, even though what normally emanates from this site are services for individual consumption.

Public consumption can both decrease and increase survival and environmental costs. Producing buses for the consumption of a public transport provider requires much less plastic, glass, metal, rubber and so on, than the production of cars to carry an equivalent number of people. Needless to say, this comparison extends to the consumption of petrol, the need for motorways and car parks, and polluting effects. Increasingly public consumption, whether for state or privately operated services for the public, is subjected to the institutional consumption of capitalism. This comes in two forms.

First there is all that is consumed in the various stages of *producing* the final product for consumption (private or public). This includes all that is consumed in producing the means (raw materials, mines, factories, machinery, tools and so on) or capital goods required for the manufacture of consumer products.[13] Some idea of the volume of capital consumption and its ecological effects is provided by James O'Connor. 'In the United States in 1987–1988, oil refining and coal products, chemicals, primary metals, and paper and pulp (all capital goods) accounted for ... 78 per cent of energy use and 88 per cent of all toxic releases.'[14]

The second form of the institutional consumption of capitalism involves all that is consumed in the various stages involved in the *circulation* and *selling* of goods – advertising, packaging, labelling, warehouses, lorries, offices, shops and so forth. What we are beginning to see is that personal and domestic consumption embodies what has already been institutionally consumed in the processes of production and circulation and *at a price that incorporates profits at each stage in these processes*. Survival costs are thus already inflated by profit.

I have said enough to suggest that strategies intent on reducing ecological demand *and* survival costs should target the institutional consumption of capitalism. We can begin to see the scope that exists for massive reductions on these fronts by considering a few examples of the unnecessary and wasteful use of vital resources that serve no other purpose than profit.

Consumption for Profit

As I argued in the previous chapter, basic necessities are no longer basic in the sense that they invariably incorporate superfluous features into their design and packaging, and are produced for a limited life (planned obsolescence). By definition, superfluous features and planned obsolescence do not enhance the use value of products, but they do enhance prices and create unnecessary ecological demands.

If industrialised production was restricted to producing *socially useful durable necessities* the savings for the environment would be significant, both in terms of the resources consumed in production and in the distribution and retailing of goods. With regard to the latter, eliminating the superfluous would remove the basis of a considerable proportion of institutional consumption currently devoured by the selling process. Furthermore, restrictions on the institutional consumption of capitalism, in theory, could mean the production of *better* and *cheaper* basic necessities. There are further potential benefits for the individual that I shall discuss later.

The superfluous finds its extreme form in luxury products for affluent consumption. But it is increasingly structured into *all* products, and consumes the energies and resources of those engaged in product design and marketing in their attempts to sell by selling fashion. The fashionable, by definition, is 'of the moment', it is short-lived, here today and gone tomorrow, and is thus an essential ingredient of accelerated obsolescence. For accelerated obsolescence we can read: 'accelerated wasteful use of resources'.

Accelerated obsolescence has become a tool of profit in more ways than one. In recent years, manufacturers and retailers have increasingly applied this tool to themselves, and in so doing have accelerated institutional consumption and with it environmental and consumer costs. The costs of the selling of goods via fashionable images has been augmented by the costs of the selling of brand names and company images that are forever undergoing revision. These costs, which are deemed necessary in order to maintain or increase a company's market share, that is profits, are transferred to the consumer and the environment.

The environmental costs of institutional consumption involved in the selling of goods are no longer confined to the established practices of the annual trading-in of car fleets, the polluting effects of hordes of salesmen scurrying around in these cars, the luxury furnishings of hotels to accommodate salesmen and so on. The growing significance of branding means that there is a more rapid turnover of the images constituting the brand image. More frequently than ever before, especially among companies experiencing, or fearing, a diminishing market share, this results in adopting a new brand image with its supporting material infrastructure and the wasteful dumping of all that materially supported the discarded image. Thus the accelerated institutional consumption associated with the refurbishment of banks, insurance companies, offices, shops and so forth. Amongst other things this involves re-building, re-decoration, new carpets to match, new furniture and equipment, new uniforms for the workforce and so on.

Now, as the proportion of profits re-invested and paid out in wages declines, and is retained for the personal consumption of the capitalist class and the highest earners, all that is consumed by the institutions of capitalism becomes increasingly geared to providing for the affluent in the form of luxury goods. It is here that the costs of branding know no limits. Producing for those who already have all that they materially need and want is to produce for a bottomless pit in which decisions to buy hardly qualify as decisions. There is nothing to 'weigh up', nothing that can make a difference. Consuming fluctuates to the rhythmless, but forever changing, beat of the fanciful and whimsical, which becomes indistinguishable from the changing images projected in the branding process. This is utterly wasteful of vital resources.

The elimination of the unnecessary and wasteful institutional con-sumption of capitalism, it is clear, would be beneficial for the environment and the consumer. But since the institutional con-sumption of capitalism provides numerous sources of profit, it is unrealistic to suppose that capitalism will voluntarily restrict itself to the production and sale of socially useful goods and durable neces-sities. Yet, unless capitalism is restricted, profit will continue to take priority over human survival.

The institutional consumption of capitalism poses, more sharply than ever before, a further contradiction that may yet lead to its demise. Quite simply, an increasing proportion of the labour time consumed by capitalism serves no other purpose than that of profit, as for example, in the form of catering to the whims of the most affluent, producing and selling goods with built-in obsolescence for mass consumption, or work in the debt industry. In other words it is labour time devoted to wasteful, useless and senseless work. Numerous surveys suggest that there is a growing desire for time to be lived rather than wasted in meaningless work.[15] The scope for meeting this desire is enormous.

As Gorz has been pointing out for some time, the use of labour-saving technology by employers has enabled an increase in output at the same time as the total volume of labour time consumed by the global economy has declined. Over the past 40 years in the advanced capitalist economies of Europe, for example, production has tripled and wealth has quadrupled. Yet only approximately 2 per cent of the working population 'carry out the whole of material production'.[16] In an egalitarian world one might expect increases in wealth to be equally shared. One might also expect labour time savings to be equally shared, and a democratically decided proportion of these savings to go into increasing jobs in socially useful work. None of this has happened. Instead, the total volume of labour time consumed has been inflated almost entirely by the non-materially productive profit industries.

Additionally, as we saw earlier, a growing element of what might be regarded as socially useful work, in health care and education for example, is rendered useless and senseless by being subjected to the dictates of the rationality derived from the profit motive. It is no accident that morale in the professions involved in socially useful work is widely reported as being at 'rock bottom'. It is no surprise, either, that throughout the workforce, the meaninglessness of senseless work more or less guarantees that, as Gorz has been pointing out for more than 20 years, workers no longer identify with their 'work'.

The existential costs of senseless work, exacerbated by the in-securities of intermittent employment, are taking their toll. It is here that the capitalist system comes to rest uneasily and stakes out the battlefield in which it seeks to claim the individual for itself, as fodder for profit. By controlling the means and conditions of survival, the capitalist system restricts individual autonomy and attempts to direct what little scope for autonomy remains into the clutches of consumerism. As I shall argue, this manipulation of autonomy approaches its existential limits as the senselessness of work becomes the norm.

Autonomy – the Battlefield

In the advanced capitalist societies a majority are surviving, perhaps not as comfortably as they would like, but they are nevertheless surviving. However an increasing number of this majority are finding the existential costs of survival intolerable. At the present time these costs are *personalised*, and tend to be expressed as the need for more time, more space, for a stress-free life and so on. These costs, in fact, reflect the *need for autonomy*.

Addressing these costs also takes a personalised form and draws on the individual's autonomy – the search for new, better-paid employment, moving, making a fresh start, divorce, a new relation-ship and so forth. The experienced success or failure of the solutions, typically understood as the responsibility of the individual, is largely a matter of luck. For the solutions are sought within the very system that spawns the problems by restricting individuals' scope for autonomy. And when the 'solutions' fail, a culture of self-blame prompts the individual to search for new solutions, or alternatively steers the individual toward personal crisis.

The need for autonomy, as I have argued elsewhere,[17] is a universal need. That this is so is based on the fact that all human beings seek more from life than mere survival, and that this 'more', if it is to be meaningful to the individual, *must be freely chosen by the individual.* In other words the meaningful life beyond survival pre-supposes the autonomy of the individual.

In capitalist society the 'more' is that of consuming beyond need. In other words, the meaningful and satisfying life, the good life, is more or less prescribed for us, as post-necessity consumption. The autonomy of individuals cannot be given free rein to decide the meaningful for themselves. Instead the meaningful is converted into one form and one form only, that of more consumption. The capitalist system reinforces this by ensuring that employed individuals are under-resourced, especially in terms of time and energy, for autonomous courses of action reflecting other, non-consumerist, expressions of the meaningful. Then the system has the audacity, as too does the latest ideology of consumerism, to refer to the consequences of this blatant material manipulation – imposed consumption – as meaningful and as the expression of individual autonomy.

Consumerism, as a substitute for autonomy, can satisfy only the most fickle. It is for the majority an inadequate compensation for the denial of a more meaningful life, but a compensation that has been tolerated in the absence of alternatives. The means (income from employment) of qualifying for this compensation not only increasingly involves the loss of time in useless and senseless labour, but it has become so insecure that the compensatory pleasures of consumerism are no longer compensatory. Nothing can compensate for a life driven and destroyed by insecurity.

Yet while we remain dependent on a system on which we can no longer depend, insecurity, and with it the undermining of autonomy, will persist, and any job, no matter how useless and senseless, will be seen as preferable to no job at all. So it is that the elimination of the unnecessary and wasteful consumption of capitalism is seen to be a bad thing because it would result in the loss of jobs. The 'thinking' here derives from the very same ideology that has it that there is no alternative to a world controlled by the power of capital, and that the world we live in is the best of all possible worlds.

Of course, it is absurd to claim that there is no alternative to capitalism. Can we not imagine a more meaningful and sensible life *for everybody,* a life that would no longer be sacrificed for the consumption of the most affluent? To even ask this question invites the accusation of 'utopianism', or, in other words: 'get real'. But, as we have seen, 'the reality' that has been created by capitalism threatens the survival of the majority and of the planet, and subordinates the autonomy of the individual to the fluctuating demands of capital. These problems are very real and will continue to be so unless we abolish capitalism, and forge a post-capitalist future that is guided by the principles of equality and autonomy.

It is beyond the scope of this book to spell out my vision of a post-capitalist future – that is another project.[18] But, it is clear that the only force capable of opposing the power of capital is *the combined power of people exerting sufficient pressure on nation-states to co-operate in the abolition of capitalism.* While the possibility of the combined power of people as an anti-capitalist force appears remote, we can be encouraged by the fact that something much less than this has moved nation-states toward a co-operative stance on abolishing Third World debt and controlling global emissions of greenhouse gases.

We can also be encouraged that the existential relevance of anti-capitalism has become a matter of some urgency. The need for autonomy, for its expansion, because of its existential relevance, can be the source of effective 'people power'. The development of this source of power is to a large extent dependent on the articulation of the existential costs of surviving and living in a consumer society as having their origins, not in the individual, but in a system that unnecessarily restricts autonomy. The individual's need for autonomy, rather than being a matter to be primarily resolved by the individual, can be addressed only by transforming the system in ways that enable an expansion of the sphere of autonomy for everyone. The arguments that I have presented throughout indicate that *this is best achieved by ensuring that survival is no longer dependent on income.*

In a world of abundance *everyone's survival should be and can be guaranteed.* To say that this is not possible or undesirable is to declare the acceptability of the inequalities, the deprivation, the insecurities and the genocide created by capitalism. A universal, sufficient and unconditional living allowance would enable people to refuse senseless employment and to live an autonomous life outside of consumerism. The successful mobilisation of people power in support of the demand for a guaranteed income would provide sufficient encouragement to mount other campaigns of existential and egalitarian relevance.

To uncouple survival from income is also to break the link between employment and income. It is here, in the field of employment, more than anywhere else, that massive gains in autonomy can be achieved by eliminating all forms of time-consuming employment that serve the unnecessary institutional consumption of capitalism, and by providing opportunities for autonomy in an expanding sphere of socially useful work.

The question arises: do we, as *individuals*, continue to chance our luck in a system that offers worsening odds of success, and in which success itself takes the form of an existentially bankrupt consumerism, or do we want a secure opportunity to live a more meaningful life? To want the latter is to *choose autonomy, individually and collectively*. Along the way we will experience the benefits of more autonomy and want even more. We will also realise that genuine autonomy (unlike consumer autonomy) is never gained at the expense of others. Or to re-phrase an insight shared by more than one luminary: no one is free until all are free.

Digression: Elitism, Adorno and Football

In Chapter 5 I noted that the Frankfurt School is widely misrepresented and criticised. In that chapter I was able to introduce my own theory of consumption by addressing some of these misrepresentations. It was not necessary for me, given my central task, to address the whole range of criticisms levelled at the Frankfurt School's critical social theory. Thus, while I acknowledged that the Frankfurt School is commonly dismissed on account of its alleged 'elitism', I allowed this to pass as I pursued more important matters.

This is not to say that judgements declaring a theory to be elitist are of no importance. Given the political correctness that pervades Cultural Studies, any theory that is judged to be elitist is automatically guaranteed short shrift. In the case of Frankfurt social theory this means that its continuing relevance for enhancing our critical understanding of social disintegration is ignored. In what follows I aim to demonstrate that references to the elitism of the Frankfurt School are totally misplaced.

The so-called 'elitism' that critics see in the writings of the Frankfurt School is specifically what might be referred to as a 'cultural elitism' that is typically associated with the exalted status of 'high culture'. Culture here is being used in the narrow sense as the world of 'letters and the arts', but is connected to culture in the broader sense, in so far as the letters and arts are traditionally associated with the lifestyle and education of those social elites who qualify as elites by virtue of their breeding.

The history of contemporary Cultural Studies is closely bound up with its opposition to cultural elitism and its institutionalisation in the Cultural Establishment. This opposition, originally intended to give legitimacy to the folk traditions of the working class – the letters and arts emanating from this class – proceeded on a number of fronts, including those of aesthetically-based criticism of some of the products of 'high' art and literature, and criticism of the instrumental use of cultural activities, such as attending operas and ballets as markers of elite social status.

The impulses to attack snobbery and the spurious grounds on which judgements are made about the merits of cultural products remain, but have far less bite in today's climate of aesthetic relativism. In this climate the whole business of aesthetic judgement has been re-ordered. Not only is it not possible to make authoritative judgements about the aesthetic merits of cultural products, but there are no authoritative grounds for judging what constitutes art in any shape or form. This has created the space for re-defining culture to incorporate popular culture, and anti-snobbery sentiments have largely been re-routed into a celebration of the standardised, mass produced dross of popular culture.

The celebratory stance toward popular culture is, within Cultural Studies, occasionally interrupted not by aesthetic criticism, but by critiques of the 'social content' of its products. Soap operas, for example, may be criticised on the grounds of sexism, racism, insensitive treatment of social issues, and so on. This does throw up real difficulties for academics within Cultural Studies. Rap music, for example, escapes criticism for its repetitiveness and lack of musical content, but invites criticism of lyrics, not in terms of inaneness, but in terms of sexism and the promotion of violence. On the other hand, there is a reluctance by some to pursue these lines of criticism. Rap music is almost entirely performed by young black men. There is an anti-elitist political correctness that forbids criticism of members of outcast social groups, such as certain ethnic and sexual minorities.

Obviously political correctness is full of contradictions, and some expressions of it are ill-considered. In its general anti-elitist form it rules out criticisms of popular culture on the grounds that these criticisms imply criticisms of 'ordinary' people, the consumers of popular culture. And this is taken to be Adorno's biggest sin – so big as to blind academics to *what he actually wrote,* so big as to make the misrepresentation of what he wrote unproblematically acceptable to those who have never read him, and so big that he can either be ignored or, alternatively, resurrected as a historical figure on which to pour ridicule and poke fun.

Adorno's anti-elitism is plain to see in *Minima Moralia* and *Negative Dialectics.*[1] But, for Cultural Studies academics, Adorno's social egalitarianism cannot be taken seriously since it was contradicted by his alleged cultural elitism. His critics wrongly assume that his criticisms of popular culture demean the working class, and they wrongly assume that he defended high culture, and thus sided with social elites. Adorno's criticisms of jazz, and, toward the end of his life, of the music of the Beatles, are mistakenly viewed as confirmation of his own bourgeois credentials.

It is unrealistic to expect Cultural Studies academics to read Adorno. (One of the reasons for the popularity of Cultural Studies is that study can proceed more by watching films or television, and listening to pop music, than by reading.) And I do not intend to read him for them. But even if the reading of Adorno is restricted to 'On Popular Music'[2] and 'The Culture Industry: Enlightenment as Mass Deception', only the most confused could possibly persist with accusing Adorno of cultural elitism.

Adorno's Marxism directed him to understanding the products of the culture industry (popular radio, popular music, popular film, popular television and so on) as being primarily determined by economic interests. The same kind of economic rationality embodied in the production of material goods for mass consumption, he argued, is evident in the production of cultural goods for mass consumption. As with material products designed for mass consumption, they are *standardised*. In other words their production obeys formulae. In the case of cultural products, standard ingredients are intended to result in a final product that will attract mass audiences. Once a successful formula has been developed, it gets repeated in ways intended to prevent audiences losing interest from the repetition of the same. Thus each 'new' product is designed to be immediatedly recognisable. The 'different' or 'novel' is merely a surface appearance of a standard underlying structure.

In developing detailed analysis of standardised cultural production, and comparing this with an equally detailed analysis of the production of more serious art forms, particularly music, Adorno identified a number of structural differences between the two types of music. In a sense, the underlying structures were presented as 'ideal types' (in the Weberian tradition) that defined each type of music and their differences from each other. Actual music could thus be judged in relation to how well it measured up to its ideal type.

However, what proved to be most upsetting to Adorno's critics was that the two ideal types reflected inbuilt values that portrayed the 'serious' or 'authentic' as superior to the 'popular'. There could be little objection to the differences between the two types of music that Adorno identified at the level of composition. Thus, for example, the emphasis in the serious type on a consistent relationship between the whole piece and each of its parts, by interwoven themes, by careful composition that reached for self-consistency and so on. Alternatively, the popular type, for example, does not require any necessary relation between the whole and its parts, change to any one part does not change the whole, there is no requirement to develop themes, but there is an emphasis on repetition. But Adorno argued that differences in the structure of composition between the two types of music promoted differences in listening responses. These differences did suggest the superiority of the serious type on aesthetic and intellectual grounds.

Adorno emphasised that a full appreciation of the serious type of music requires effort, both in terms of powers of concentration and engagement that enables a thoughtful experiencing of the whole piece. By contrast, the popular type, which contains cues for prompting automatic responses, can be enjoyed with little effort and thought, and the sources of enjoyment are not confined to musical quality, but can vary from a dance-inspiring beat, for example, to admiration of the energy or style of the performer(s).

Adorno's analysis of the two ideal types of music was published in the 1940s, at a time when, unlike today, thinking and the development of the intellect were positively valued. While it strikes me as quite unremarkable that popular music has little to offer to thinking and the intellect, critics of Adorno have seen such a judgement as one that implies a condemnation of the working class. It implies no such thing. The working class has plenty to think about as it is. Adorno recognised this, and also recognised that whatever the intention of the producers of standardised products, cultural or otherwise, people 'could see through them'.

In the 'Culture Industry ...' essay, written with Horkheimer, which is roundly condemned for portraying a disparaging view of the intelligence of ordinary people, Adorno and Horkheimer refer to the culture industry forcing its products on 'a resistant public'.[3] Similarly they refer to consumers' 'double mistrust of traditional culture as ideology' which is 'combined with mistrust of industrialized culture as a swindle'. They go on to argue that the products of the latter 'are secretly rejected by the fortunate recipients'.[4] Earlier in the essay they note: 'That the differences between the Chrysler range and General Motors products is basically illusory strikes every child with a keen interest in varieties.'[5] Now, it is obvious that these statements (and there are many more) indicate something other than the view that the recipients of popular music are essentially an unthinking mass.

We can surely make statements about the potential aesthetic and intellectual value of all sorts of resources, musical or otherwise, without implying that our use of these resources, for whatever reason, reveals fundamental truths about our intellects and aesthetic sensibilities. Further, aesthetic and intellectual resources are numerous, and are not confined to cultural products. It seems to me that Adorno's critics have been quite careless in jumping to unwarranted conclusions.

It is perfectly legitimate to attempt to distinguish between two ideal types of music in terms of structure of composition and the kinds of listening promoted by the different structures. It may well be the case that socialisation and social circumstances strongly influence both the role of music in an individual's life, and particular musical tastes. But it is not legitimate to assume that these tastes exhaust all that can be said about a person's intellect. This was not Adorno's project. In misreading Adorno in this way critics miss the whole point of his critique of popular culture.

That this is so can be made apparent by a playful application of Adorno's analysis of music to football. It would be a fairly simple matter for me to draw a distinction between two ideal types of football: 'pure' or 'total' football on the one hand, and 'standardised' or 'safety-first' football on the other. Differences between these two types of football can be made in terms of what is required for their execution (production) and for their appreciation (reception). Standardised football is immediatedly recognised as embodying the standard ingredients that many spectators associate with entertainment. Its production stems from the commercialisation of professional football: lack of success courts the risk of financial difficulties for clubs, and this leads to a mentality dominated by the fear of losing. Hence the development of a safety-first approach to assuage this fear.

The fan understands this well and judges his or her team in how successful they are at avoiding defeat. Players are spontaneously (automatically) applauded for their physical efforts and automatically chastised for taking unnecessary risks, especially when attempting to display outrageous skill that does not come off. The fan attends a match equipped with a number of automatic, unthinking and often moronic responses that can be spontaneously elicited by cues from the game. Young children and amateur teams imitate the safety-first model. Thus those that go on to become professionals already belong to the industry before they become stars.[6]

In sharp contrast, pure or total football demands more in the way of skill and thought from players. It is not automatically associated with success, although it is associated with the more memorable and inspirational teams. (Hungary and Holland were beaten World Cup finalists in 1954 and 1974 respectively, and the Brazilians of 1982 failed to qualify for the final.) Only a few of the most thoughtful and skilful teams have been regularly successful against well-drilled safety-first teams. The appreciation of total football requires a mentality that is radically different from that which is able to find entertainment in standardised safety-first football. It values possession of the ball as opposed to 'getting rid' of it, or launching it willy-nilly into the opponent's penalty area. It demands an appreciation of the movement of players that enables a team to retain possession of the ball, and this requires an ability to see the display of individual skill in the context of the movement of the whole team. It understands skilful play as a collective, rather than an exclusively individual, accomplishment. It promotes an enjoyment of the game that is based more on the team's ability to achieve total football than on the result.

In a football culture in which safety-first football defines how the game should be played, the young, skilful, thoughtful and collectively-minded player has no future as a professional unless he can curb his 'purer' instincts and display the standard attributes required in the game.

I could go on, and on, but I have said enough to make my point. My distinction between pure football and standardised football is the equivalent of Adorno's distinction between serious and popular music. In both, the distinction is made to emphasise the different values they serve. Both acknowledge the negative impact of economic interests on aesthetic and intellectual resources. Commercial interests are dominant in defining the popular, but they also contaminate the not so popular. Adorno, himself a composer, reserved his strongest critical venom for music that took on the mantle of the serious, but actually fell way short of his ideal type. Likewise, I could just as easily criticise successful football teams that wrongly assume that their success reflects their ability to play total football.

Adorno can be accused of a specifically defined musical elitism. I can be accused of football elitism. No doubt the most muddled would not hesitate in accusing me of cultural elitism, and I could provide fuel for their confused minds were I to elaborate a little on

the mindlessness and utter ignorance displayed by many football fans, and how this is given legitimacy on popular radio in the form of increasing amounts of air time devoted to 'phone-ins'. However, because the ignorance and mindlessness of football fans bears no relation to their social or occupational background, it would be impossible to extend my football elitism into a cultural elitism.

This brings me to the source of error committed by critics of Adorno. My distinction between pure and standardised football does not lend itself to being (mis)interpreted as a reflection of values peculiar to an established social or cultural elite. Football, after all, is the people's game. But Adorno wrote about music rather than football. Adorno's distinction between serious and popular music as ideal types is ignored. Rather, 'the serious' is wrongly translated as a euphemism for the tastes of elite culture.

Notes and References

Introduction

1. Most of the major issues involved in the distinction between needs and wants are clearly discussed in: L. Doyal and I. Gough, *A Theory of Human Need* (London: Macmillan, 1991); D. Slater, *Consumer Culture and Modernity* (Cambridge: Polity Press, 1997); and K. Soper, *On Human Needs: Open and Closed Theories in a Marxist Perspective* (Sussex: The Harvester Press, 1981).

Chapter: 1 The Latest Ideology of Consumerism

1. Theories emphasising the power of capital remain dominant in Marxist critical social theory. In economic theory, econometric-based theories are dominant. See B. Fine, M. Heasman and J. Wright, *Consumption in the Age of Affluence: The World of Food* (London: Routledge, 1996).
2. H. Mackay (ed.), *Consumption and Everyday Life* (London: Sage, 1997) p. 3.
3. Ibid.
4. Ibid.
5. Ibid.
6. Ibid., p. 6.
7. An internal account of the early history of Cultural Studies is provided by Stuart Hall, 'Cultural Studies and the Centre: some problematics and problems', in S. Hall, D. Hobson, A. Lowe and P. Willis (eds), *Culture, Media, Language* (London: Hutchinson, 1980) pp. 15–47. See also J. McGuigan, *Cultural Populism* (London: Routledge, 1992). For a progressive and highly critical history see R. Jacoby, *The End of Utopia: Politics and Culture in an Age of Apathy* (New York: Basic Books, 1999).
8. Cultural Studies as it is known today originated in the founding of the Centre for Contemporary Cultural Studies at the University of Birmingham, England, in 1964.
9. See for example, R. Jessop, K. Bonnett, S. Bromley and T. Ling, *Thatcherism: A Tale of Two Nations* (Cambridge: Polity Press, 1988).
10. The seminal work here is that of N. Abercrombie, S. Hill and B.S. Turner, *The Dominant Ideology Thesis* (London: Allen and Unwin, 1980).
11. Especially influential were: A. Gramsci in Q. Hoare and G. Nowell Smith (eds), *Selections from the Prison Notebooks* (London: Lawrence and Wishart, 1971), and L. Althusser, *Essays on Ideology* (London: Verso, 1984).
12. J. Lacan, *Écrits: A Selection* (London: Tavistock, 1977).
13. F. Mort, 'The Politics of Consumption', in S. Hall and M. Jacques (eds), *New Times: The Changing Face of Politics in the 1990s* (London: Lawrence and Wishart, 1989) p. 167.

14. For example: F. Bowring, 'Job scarcity: the perverted form of a potential blessing', *Sociology*, vol. 31: 1 (1999) pp. 69–84; A. Gorz, *Critique of Economic Reason* (London: Verso, 1989); A. Gorz, *Capitalism, Socialism, Ecology* (London: Verso, 1994); A. Gorz, *Reclaiming Work: Beyond the Wage-Based Society* (Cambridge: Polity Press, 1999).

15. Z. Bauman, *Intimations of Postmodernity* (London: Routledge, 1992) p. 49.

16. Ibid., p. 51.

17. J. Baudrillard, *Selected Writings* (Cambridge: Polity Press, 1988).

18. J. Baudrillard, *The Consumer Society: Myths and Structures* (London: Sage, 1998) p. 72.

19. The most radical and comprehensive critiques come from the few Marxists sufficiently bothered to address ideas fielded as new, but which actually are defeated ideas resurrected from the past. See A. Callinicos, *Against Postmodernism: A Marxist Critique* (Cambridge: Polity Press, 1989). One of the reasons for being bothered is that postmodern discourses are reflected in current social policies. For an excellent critique of the latter, see M. Sanders, D. Hill and E. Hankin, 'Education Theory and the Return to Class Analysis', in D. Hill, P. McLaren, M. Cole and G. Rikowski (eds), *Postmodernism in Educational Theory* (London: the Tufnell Press, 1999) pp. 98–130.

20. J. Baudrillard, *For a Critique of the Political Economy of the Sign* (St Louis, MO: Telos, 1981).

21. J.-F. Lyotard, *The Postmodern Condition: A Report on Knowledge* (Minneapolis: University of Minnesota Press, 1984). A brief extract from this book appears as 'The Postmodern Condition', in J.C. Alexander and S. Seidman (eds), *Culture and Society: Contemporary Debates* (Cambridge: Cambridge University Press, 1990) pp. 330–41.

22. Ibid., p. 339.

23. I am thinking here of the Research Assessment Exercise (RAE) which is used by government to award funds to universities. Lecturers are required to publish a minimum *number* of publications every five years. A short article in an academic journal, for example, counts as one publication, as too does one lengthy book. As a consequence there has been a proliferation of new academic journals to accommodate the growing *volume* of writing. The pressure continuously to publish, whether or not one has anything to say, has contributed to priority being given to writing – writing *anything* – and thus to the decline of reading and contemplation. This deterioration in the intellectual quality of academic journals is reinforced by academic promotions policies that distribute rewards on the basis of an academic's compliance with the quantitative standards of the RAE. And, in the absence of commonly agreed standards for assessing the *quality* of an academic's work, and thus promotion reflecting qualitative judgements, universities have created an ethos of self-promotion which opens the floodgates of opportunity for those who can 'shout the most and loudest', that is for those who best satisfy *quantitative* criteria. Little wonder that professorships are regularly awarded for unremarkable 'achievement'.

Chapter 2: The Symbolic Value of Consumption

1. R. Barthes, *Mythologies* (London: Jonathan Cape, 1972).
2. For example, R. Hebdige, *Subculture: The Meaning of Style* (London: Methuen, 1979), and P. Willis, *Profane Culture* (London: Routledge, 1978).
3. J. Fiske, *Reading the Popular* (London: Unwin Hyman, 1989) p. 14.
4. J. Fiske, *Understanding Popular Culture* (London: Unwin Hyman, 1989) p. 37.
5. M. Featherstone, 'Postmodernism and the Aestheticization of Everyday Life', in S. Lash and J. Friedman (eds), *Modernity and Identity* (Oxford: Blackwell, 1992) p. 270.
6. Ibid.
7. Ibid.
8. Ibid., p. 269.
9. M. Sahlins, 'Food as Symbolic Code', in J.C. Alexander and S. Seidman (eds), *Culture and Society: Contemporary Debates* (Cambridge: Cambridge University Press, 1990) p. 94.
10. Ibid., p. 95.
11. Ibid., p. 99.
12. A commonly repeated claim, forcibly expressed in H. Mackay (ed.), *Consumption and Everyday Life* (London: Sage, 1997).
13. M. de Certeau, *The Practice of Everyday Life* (Berkeley: California University Press, 1984).
14. C. Campbell, *The Romantic Ethic and the Spirit of Modern Consumerism* (Oxford: Blackwell, 1989).
15. G. Ritzer, *Enchanting a Disenchanted World: Revolutionizing the Means of Consumption* (London: Pine Forge Press, 1999) p. 194.
16. Ibid., p. 195.
17. M. Featherstone, *Consumer Culture and Postmodernism* (London: Sage, 1991) p. 66.
18. Ibid., p. 67.
19. Ibid., p. 24.
20. Ibid., p. 95.
21. For example, Mackay *Consumption*.

Chapter 3: Consumption, Identity and Lifestyle

1. H. Mackay (ed.), *Consumption and Everyday Life* (London: Sage, 1997), p. 4.
2. D. Miller, 'Consumption and its Consequences', in Mackay, *Consumption*, p. 19.
3. R. Bocock, *Consumption* (London: Routledge, 1993) p. 112.
4. T. Veblen, *The Theory of the Leisure Class: An Economic Study of Institutions* (London: Unwin Books, 1970).
5. P. Bourdieu, *Distinction: A Social Critique of the Judgement of Taste* (London: Routledge, 1984).
6. M. Lamont, *Money, Morals and Manners: The Culture of the French and the American Upper-Middle Class* (Chicago: University of Chicago Press, 1992)

pp. 182–3, cited in C. Lury, *Consumer Culture* (Cambridge: Polity Press, 1996) p. 109.

7. Z. Bauman, *The Individualized Society* (Cambridge: Polity Press, 2001).
8. See for example, A. Giddens, *Modernity and Self-Identity: Self and Society in the Late Modern Age* (Cambridge: Polity Press, 1991).
9. C. Leadbetter, 'Power to the Person', in S. Hall and M. Jacques (eds), *New Times: The Changing Face of Politics in the 1990s* (London: Lawrence and Wishart, 1989) p. 140.
10. S. Hall, 'The Meaning of New Times', in Hall and Jacques *New Times*, p. 131.
11. F. Mort, 'The Politics of Consumption', in Hall and Jacques *New Times*, p. 170.
12. Lury *Consumer Culture*, p. 255.
13. C. Lodziak, *Manipulating Needs: Capitalism and Culture* (London: Pluto Press, 1995) pp. 12–19.
14. Lury *Consumer Culture*, p. 197.
15. P. Willis, *Common Culture* (Milton Keynes: Open University Press, 1990) p. 139.
16. S. Ewen, 'Marketing Dreams: The Political Elements of Style', in A. Tomlinson (ed.), *Consumption, Identity, and Style: Marketing, Meanings, and the Packaging of Pleasure* (London: Routledge, 1990) p. 43.
17. Ibid., p. 45.
18. Ibid.
19. Ibid., p. 46.
20. Ibid., pp. 51–2.
21. Lury *Consumer Culture*, pp. 196–7.
22. S. Redhead, *The End-of-the-Century Party: Youth and Pop Towards 2000* (Manchester: Manchester University Press, 1990) p. 89, quoted in Lury *Consumer Culture*, p. 213.
23. Willis *Common Culture*, p. 26.
24. R.D. Laing, *The Divided Self: An Existential Study in Sanity and Madness* (Harmondsworth: Penguin Books, 1965).
25. Giddens *Modernity and Self-Identity*, p. 198.
26. Z. Bauman, *Legislators and Interpreters* (Cambridge: Polity Press, 1989) p. 189, quoted in Giddens *Modernity and Self-Identity*, p. 198.
27. Bauman *Legislators,* and *Freedom* (Milton Keynes: Open University Press, 1988).
28. Bauman *Legislators,* p. 189.
29. Giddens *Modernity and Self-Identity*, p. 198.
30. Ibid., p. 5.
31. Ibid., p. 81.
32. Ibid., p. 5.
33. I have argued this point in *Manipulating Needs,* especially pp. 73–91. Various organisations such as MIND, The Mental Health Foundation, the Worldwatch Institute, and the WHO, from time to time publish alarming statistics on mental health. In 2000, for example, it was reported that 8 million people in Britain were being medically treated for a mental health problem, and that 20 million people were prescribed anti-depressants. While anti-depressants are routinely prescribed for all sorts of

conditions, it is widely noted that depressive-anxiety disorders account for the majority of mental health problems. A person in their mid-twenties is ten times more likely to suffer from depression today than was the case 50 years ago. In the US it has been calculated that between 40 and 60 per cent of the population is 'mentally ill' in any one year!
34. C. Lasch, *The Minimal Self: Psychic Survival in Troubled Times* (London: Picador, 1985) p. 38.

Chapter 4: Consumption as Freedom

1. Z. Bauman, *Intimations of Postmodernity* (London: Routledge, 1992) p. 51.
2. J. McGuigan, *Cultural Populism* (London: Routledge, 1992), p. 119.
3. A. Gorz, *Reclaiming Work: Beyond the Wage-Based Society* (Cambridge: Polity Press, 1999), p. 15.
4. Z. Bauman, *The Individualized Society* (Cambridge: Polity Press, 2001) p. 114. The report in question is that of the United Nations Development Programme published in 1998.
5. A.G. Frank, *Capitalism and Under-development in Latin America* (New York: Monthly Review Press, 1969).
6. Bauman *Individualized Society*, p. 114.
7. Quoted in E. Dore, 'Debt and ecological disaster in Latin America', *Race and Class*, vol. 34: 1 (1992) p. 85. Dore notes that 'in his defence', the World Bank vice-president said the memo was in a form that 'deprived [his comments] of their original, highly ironic context'.
8. Z. Bauman, *In Search of Politics* (Cambridge: Polity Press, 1999) p. 68.
9. A. Gorz, *Strategy for Labour: A Radical Proposal* (Boston: Beacon Press, 1967) p. 68.
10. Ibid., p. 90.
11. Bauman *In Search of Politics*, p. 68.
12. N. Chomsky, *The Common Good* (Chicago: Odonian Press, 1998) p. 14.
13. C. Lasch, *The Minimal Self: Psychic Survival in Troubled Times* (London: Picador, 1985), p. 38.
14. Bauman *In Search of Politics,* p. 72.
15. Ibid., pp. 72–3.
16. Ibid., p. 73.
17. N. Whiteley, *Design for Society* (London: Reaktion Books, 1993) p. 37.

Chapter 5: Compelled to Consume

1. M. Featherstone, *Consumer Culture and Postmodernism* (London: Sage, 1991), p. 14.
2. Ibid.
3. See N. Abercrombie, S. Hill and B.S. Turner, *The Dominant Ideology Thesis* (London: Allen and Unwin, 1980). Cultural Studies has only belatedly become open to such evidence. For almost 20 years Cultural Studies ignored all the evidence reviewed by Michael Mann's, 'The social cohesion of liberal democracy', *American Sociological Review*, vol. 35 (1970) pp. 423–39.

4. Featherstone *Consumer Culture*, p. 15.
5. H. Marcuse, *One Dimensional Man* (London: Abacus, 1972) p. 21.
6. A. Gorz, *Strategy for Labour: A Radical Proposal* (Boston: Beacon Press, 1967), p. 71.
7. J. McGuigan, *Cultural Populism* (London: Routledge, 1992), p. 121.
8. T. Adorno and M. Horkheimer, *Dialectic of Enlightenment* (London: Verso, 1979) pp. 120–67. This was originally published in 1944.
9. Ibid., p. 122.
10. Ibid., p. 37.
11. T. Adorno, *Negative Dialectics* (New York: Continuum, 1973) p. 190.
12. Ibid.
13. A. Gorz, *Critique of Economic Reason* (London: Verso, 1989) pp. 153–64.
14. Ibid., pp. 141–2, and A. Gorz, *Capitalism, Sociology, Ecology* (London: Verso, 1994) pp. 44–52.
15. A. Gorz, *Reclaiming Work: Beyond the Wage-Based Society* (Cambridge: Polity Press, 1999) pp. 77–8.
16. Gorz *Critique of Economic Reason*, p. 117.
17. Ibid.
18. Adorno and Horkheimer *Dialectic of Enlightenment*, pp. 152–3.
19. Federal Trade Commission, *Annual Report 1997*, Washington.
20. See for example the studies reported by Gorz *Re-Claiming Work*, pp. 60–4, and by F. Bowring, 'Job scarcity: the perverted form of a potential blessing', *Sociology*, vol. 31: 1 (1999) pp. 80–1. See also: R.E. Lane, 'Markets and the satisfaction of human wants', *Journal of Economic Issues*, vol. 12 (1978) pp. 799–827. Confirmation of Lane's findings, that after taking care of necessity most people prioritise values that cannot be addressed via consumption, is to be found predominantly in studies of attitudes toward work. Increasingly more people are voicing a need for time. Increasingly, too, more people are seeking reduced working hours even if this means a reduced income. See A. Hayden, *Sharing the Work, Sparing the Planet: Work Time, Consumption, and Ecology* (London: Zed Books, 1999) pp. 176–82.
21. One of the few studies is that of H. Sahin and J.P. Robinson, 'Beyond the realm of necessity: television and the colonization of leisure', *Media, Culture and Society*, vol. 3 (1980) pp. 85–95. One of their survey findings was that television viewing 'emerges as the most expendable or least important of daily activities' (p. 93).

Chapter 6: Compelled to Consume More

1. A. Gorz, *Reclaiming Work: Beyond the Wage-Based Society* (Cambridge: Polity Press, 1999), p. 89, and C. Offe, *Modernity and the State: East, West* (Cambridge: Polity Press, 1996) p. 122.
2. Eurostat (the EU statistical service), reported in the *Guardian*, 21 November 1997.
3. W. Hutton, *The State We're In* (London: Vintage, 1996) pp. 106–8.
4. Ibid., p. 106.
5. Ibid., p. 108.

6. Office for National Statistics, *Social Trends* (2001).
7. *Labour Research*, February 1997.
8. Gorz *Reclaiming Work*, p. 17.
9. Ibid.
10. J.K. Galbraith, *The Culture of Contentment* (Harmondsworth: Penguin Books, 1992) pp. 55–6.
11. Gorz *Reclaiming Work*, p. 17.
12. W. Greider, *One World, Ready or Not: The Manic Logic of Global Capitalism* (Harmondsworth: Allen Lane, 1997) p. 197.
13. A. Giddens, *The Third Way: The Renewal of Social Democracy* (Cambridge: Polity Press, 1998) pp. 148–9. Giddens writes:

    > Of the trillion US dollars' worth of currencies exchanged every day, only 5 per cent relate to trade and other substantive economic transactions. The other 95 per cent is made up of speculations and arbitrages, as traders wielding huge sums look for rapid profits on exchange rate fluctuations and interest rate differentials ... Portfolio capital has spectacular mobility – hundreds of billions of 'hot money' can desert a market in one day.

14. Gorz *Reclaiming Work*, p. 18. Gorz notes that Nike, when manufacturing in the Philippines, paid their 14 American board members 'an annual income equal to the wages of 18,000 women workers'.
15. This argument has been made with great clarity by both Gorz and Offe. See A. Gorz, *Strategy for Labour: A Radical Proposal* (Boston: Beacon Press, 1967) pp. 76–94, and C. Offe, *Contradictions of the Welfare State* (London: Hutchinson, 1984) pp. 224–7; *Disorganized Capitalism: Contemporary Transformations of Work and Politics* (Cambridge: Polity Press, 1985) pp. 120–4; and *Modernity and the State*, pp. 121–46.
16. Gorz *Strategy for Labour*, p. 80.
17. F. Bowring, 'Job scarcity: the perverted form of a potential blessing', *Sociology*, vol. 31: 1 (1999) p. 79.
18. Ibid.
19. Gorz *Reclaiming Work*, pp. 27–8.
20. The exception would appear to be Denmark. See Gorz *Reclaiming Work*, pp. 19–20.
21. See Hutton *The State We're In*, pp. 197–203.
22. Giddens *Third Way*, p. 113.
23. Adapted (and updated) from E. Papadakis and P. Taylor-Gooby, *The Private Provision of Public Welfare: State, Market and Community* (Sussex: Wheatsheaf Books, 1987) p. 156.
24. Ibid., p. 145. Today's figure of 30 per cent is based on estimations supplied by the National Federation of Housing Associations.
25. For a comprehensive review of the research on health hazards in modern homes see J. Ashton and R. Laura, *The Perils of Progress: The Health and Environment Hazards of Modern Technology and What You Can Do About Them* (London: Zed Books, 1999).
26. S. Irvine and A. Ponton, *A Green Manifesto: Policies for a Green Future* (London: Macdonald Optima, 1988) p. 34.

27. Hutton *The State We're In*, p. 73.
28. Offe *Modernity and the State*, pp. 126–8.
29. The wholly unscientific and spurious nature of psychometric testing is discussed in C. Lodziak, *The Power of Television: A Critical Appraisal* (London: Frances Pinter, 1986) pp. 13–18.
30. Gorz *Reclaiming Work*, p. 51. Gorz refers to the findings of a European Commission survey.
31. Ibid.
32. Ibid.

Chapter 7: Consumption for What?

1. W. Greider, *One World, Ready or Not: The Manic Logic of Global Capitalism* (Harmondsworth: Allen Lane, 1997) p. 81–102.
2. Ibid., p. 220.
3. Ibid., p. 321.
4. A. Gorz, *Reclaiming Work: Beyond the Wage-Based Society* (Cambridge: Polity Press, 1999) p. 19.
5. Ibid.
6. E. Dore, 'Debt and ecological disaster in Latin America', Race and Class, vol. 34: 1 (1992) p. 73.
7. Ibid., p. 74.
8. P. Donovan, 'One Step Forward, Two Steps Back!', *Morning Star*, 12 June 1999.
9. S. George, *Ill Fares the Land: Essays on Food, Hunger and Power* (Harmondsworth: Penguin Books, 1990) p. 231.
10. C.B. Macpherson, *The Rise and Fall of Economic Justice and Other Essays* (Oxford: Oxford University Press, 1987) p. 21.
11. Reported in *Le Monde*, 12 March 1996, quoted by V. Forrester, *The Economic Horror* (Cambridge: Polity Press, 1999) pp. 98–9.
12. George *Ill Fares the Land*, p. 223.
13. See Karl Marx, *Capital: A Critique of Political Economy*, Volume 2 (London: Lawrence and Wishart, 1956) pp. 399–402.
14. J. O'Connor, *Natural Causes: Essays in Ecological Marxism* (New York: The Guildford Press, 1998) p. 182.
15. See A. Hayden, *Sharing the Work, Spring the Planet: Work Time, Consumption, and Ecology* (London: Zed Books, 1999).
16. Gorz *Reclaiming Work*.
17. C. Lodziak, *Manipulating Needs: Capitalism and Culture* (London: Pluto Press, 1995).
18. A post-capitalist future oriented to maximising individual and collective autonomy (true democracy) pre-supposes a protected egalitarian world order. There are a number of anti-capitalist policies that strike me as most relevant in this regard. Gorz has provided the most comprehensive defence of the need for a *universal* and unconditional living allowance. See Gorz *Reclaiming Work*, pp. 80–93. See also Z. Bauman, *In Search of Politics* (Cambridge: Polity Press, 1999) pp. 180–97, and C. Offe, *Modernity and the State: East, West* (Cambridge: Polity Press, 1996) pp. 201–21. Both

Bauman and Gorz recognise the need for nation-states to agree to co-operate in establishing a universal income. For me this translates into the need for a non-capitalist regulator of global capitalism.

The regulation of global capitalism is also required in order to secure *binding agreements* on measures to create a 'level playing field'. Such measures include, for example, compensation to Third World societies (abolition of debt is a first step), returning land and other resources in under-nourished societies (see A. Gorz, *Paths to Paradise: On the Liberation from Work* (London: Pluto Press, 1985) pp. 3–5), regulating trade to obey the norm of 'a fair swap' rather than the profit interests of the powerful, and policies of global taxation on profits, on unnecessary production, on pollution and so on.

All of these kinds of measures would not only enable the installation of a universal living allowance, but would, with this, enable individuals to participate collectively in decisions that most affect the conditions of their lives. Such decisions range from deciding what to produce, socially and for oneself, the redistribution of socially useful work and working time, to decisions about the physical organisation of our communities and cities.

Digression: Elitism, Adorno and Football

1. T. Adorno, *Minima Moralia: Reflections from Damaged Life* (London: Verso, 1978) and *Negative Dialectics* (New York; Continuum, 1973).
2. Adorno (with the assistance of G. Simpson), 'On popular music', *Studies in Philosophy and Social Science*, vol. 9, no. 1 (1941). An accurate and accessible summary of this paper is presented by D. Held, *Introduction to Critical Theory: Horkheimer to Habermas* (London: Hutchinson, 1980) pp. 96–105.
3. T. Adorno and M. Horkheimer, 'The Culture Industry: Enlightenment as Mass Deception', in Adorno and Horkheimer, *Dialectic of Enlightenment* (London: Verso, 1979), pp.120–67. Originally published in 1944.
4. Ibid., p. 161.
5. Ibid., p. 123.
6. Ibid., p. 122. Adorno and Horkheimer note that 'talented performers belong to the [culture] industry long before it displays them; otherwise they would not be so eager to fit in'.

Index

177